PATCHWORK BABY

To Thomas and Nathan

. . . and to Munni Srivastava for her inspiration and ideas and not least her sewing skills when time was pressing, and to Bill for his patience and encouragement over the months . . . and the countless cups of tea.

Christine Donaldson, January 1994

Peta Ewins, our 'patchwork baby'.

PATCHWORK
BABY

Original Patchwork & Quilted Designs
CHRISTINE DONALDSON

LITTLE, BROWN AND COMPANY

BOSTON · NEW YORK · TORONTO · LONDON

ACKNOWLEDGEMENTS

The producers and the author of this book would like to thank their little models – Hetty Touquet, Peta Ewins, Rosanna Anness, Juliet Amoruso, Emma Brown and Alexander Osborne – who put up with flashlights and changes of clothes with so much good grace and happy gurgles. Thanks are also due to their respective mothers who brought them to be photographed or allowed us to photograph them in their own homes. Last but not least, Mrs Gudrun Garbe who acted as 'godmother' to Peta when we came to photograph the christening robe. Between them, they made the clothes come to life.

A special thank you to the cover model: Hetty Touquet.

A LITTLE, BROWN BOOK

First published in Great Britain in 1994
by Little, Brown and Company

A CIP catalogue record for this book
is available from the British Library

ISBN 0-316-90700-6

10 9 8 7 6 5 4 3 2 1

Conceived, produced and designed by
SAVITRI BOOKS LTD
115J Cleveland Street
London W1P 5PN

Art direction and design by Mrinalini Srivastava
Edited by Caroline Taggart
Main photography by Matthew Chattle
Special photography by Sue Baker and Françoise Legrand

Phototypeset in Souvenir Light by Dorchester Typesetting Group, Dorset, England
Colour origination produced by Mandarin Offset, Hong Kong
Printed and bound in Spain by Cayfosa Industria Grafica, Barcelona

Little, Brown and Company (UK) Ltd
Brettenham House
Lancaster Place
London WC2E 7EN

NOTES ON COPYRIGHT

Contents

Introduction

Making baby clothes and dainty nursery accessories is sheer delight and part and parcel of the joy of expecting a child or grandchild. It is an ancestral tradition and the therapeutic and calming effects of sewing are well known.

I have tried to assemble a selection of objects to suit a variety of tastes and skills. Some of the clothes, such as the silk dress and rompers, have been made in traditional pastel colours; others – the Seminole jackets or the dungarees, for instance – are in bright, trendy colours. The range of nursery accessories has also been designed on the same principle. Some of the items are modest and can be made by a beginner or as a small gift to a friend, yet because they are personal and a good deal of thought has gone into their design and making, they are special. Others require a greater investment in time, money and skill. The christening robe, for instance, was designed as a family heirloom and it is well worth spending a good deal of time on it. Most of the projects, however, were designed keeping firmly in mind the busy lives most women live today.

Wherever necessary, metric measurements and quantities have been adapted to ensure that the projects are workable in imperial, and vice versa. This is not only to cater for those readers who live in countries where imperial measurements are the norm, but also for the benefit of makers on this side of the Atlantic who still 'think in inches'.

Working with patchwork is not an exact science. Slight inaccuracies in sewing, while they do not alter the overall effect of the patchwork, can add up gradually and throw all your measurements out of kilter. To avoid this, I advise producing the piece of patchwork first, then using it as a 'template' to cut corresponding panels or strips or plain fabric borders. This method avoids a lot of heartache.

In the 'shopping list' at the beginning of each project, I have specified the amounts of base fabric you need to buy (most of the objects are decorated with patchwork rather than made entirely out of patchwork). The exceptions to the rule are projects for which exact quantities cannot be given as they will depend on the size of the individual objects you want to cover – the Moses and toiletry baskets, for instance.

For the patchwork, I have given a guideline to quantities of fabric required, as you will probably want to use fabrics you already have and buy remnants or small quantities of cloth to widen your palette. Remember that in patchwork a small piece goes a long way and that investing in a few centimetres or inches of an exciting, possibly expensive, material will pay dividends when you see the finished result!

When you make baby clothes, remember that age in relation to size is often deceptive. Measure the child and compare with the measurements specified in the project to ensure that the clothes will fit and that you allow for 'growing space'. If you spend a good deal of time making something special, it is wise to ensure that it will fit for as long as possible – babies grow so fast.

One final word of advice: always test for colour fastness and shrinkage by washing the fabrics before you start on your piece of patchwork; and if you use deep-coloured silk for something really spectacular, have the item dry-cleaned.

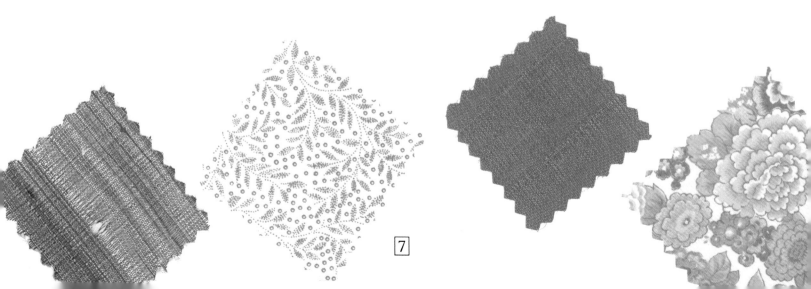

Her First Party Dress

This cream jacquard silk dress is trimmed with a Dresden Plate Patchwork border on the skirt and the bodice. The top of the dress is entirely lined in cream pongé silk and is trimmed with narrow lace at the neck. The underskirt is also made of pongé, while a second underskirt – made of fine tulle and edged with the same narrow lace – just peeps out from under the skirt.

This dress is exquisite enough to form part of a christening outfit, in which case you can make a matching bonnet such as the one shown on page 119, trimming it with a length of Dresden Plate border. The dress is classical in design and will not date. The beauty of the materials used, coupled with the time and effort spent on it, will produce what could become a family heirloom. The pattern gives measurements for 6-, 12- and 18-month-old girls but, as always, measure your child – babies of the same age can vary a great deal in size. There is a matching boy's romper suit on page 18.

YOU WILL NEED

Main dress fabric:
jacquard silk or raw silk, cotton lawn, cotton and polyester mix

Size:		6 months	12 months	18 months
Fabric width:	115 cm	1.10 m	1.30 m	1.40 m
	45 in	1¼ yd	1½ yd	1⅝ yd
	150 cm	0.90 m	1.10 m	1.15 m
	60 in	1 yd	1¼ yd	1⅜ yd

Lining: silk pongé or fine lawn, synthetic lining – same quantities as given for the dress fabric

Underskirt: 1 m/1¼ yd of fine tulle

Narrow lace: 2.5 m/3 yd   Narrow ribbon: 1.5 m/1¼ yd
2 small buttons   Matching thread
                    Stiff paper and cardboard for templates

This cream-coloured jacquard silk dress is modelled by Peta on the first page of this book. Depending on the fabrics you select for the patchwork, the dress is hand-washable, using soap flakes or any delicate-fabric type product. Do not wring. Smooth patchwork into position while wet and allow to drip-dry on a hanger.

The back of the dress. The bodice has 2 small mother-of-pearl buttons and the back of the waist is tied with a bow of the narrow ribbon. The hem of the skirt has been lifted to reveal the tulle underskirt, edged with lace.

inner template: paper
outer template: cloth

**Cut 90 paper templates
and 90 fabric pieces.**

For the patchwork: 25 cm (¼ yd) of 6 different fabrics. I used raw silk for the 2 plain colours and tiny Liberty prints for the rest.

1) Using the inner portion of the pattern opposite, make a master template out of cardboard and cut 90 paper templates. Refer to instructions for Dresden Plate Patchwork on page 129.

2) Using the outer measurements of the pattern, which include the seam allowance, make a master template out of cardboard and cut 15 pieces each out of your 6 coloured and printed fabrics.

3) Following instructions on page 129, make up the skirt border, using 72 pieces of patchwork. You will need to assemble 10 pieces for the front of the bodice, and 4 pieces for each side of the back of the bodice.

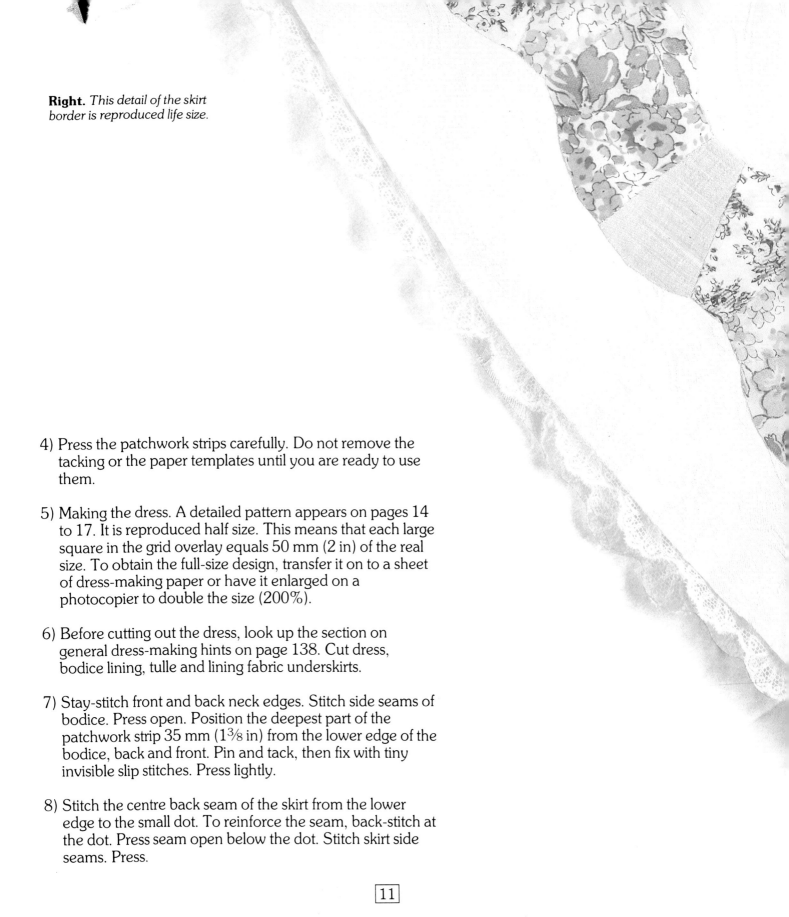

Right. *This detail of the skirt border is reproduced life size.*

4) Press the patchwork strips carefully. Do not remove the tacking or the paper templates until you are ready to use them.

5) Making the dress. A detailed pattern appears on pages 14 to 17. It is reproduced half size. This means that each large square in the grid overlay equals 50 mm (2 in) of the real size. To obtain the full-size design, transfer it on to a sheet of dress-making paper or have it enlarged on a photocopier to double the size (200%).

6) Before cutting out the dress, look up the section on general dress-making hints on page 138. Cut dress, bodice lining, tulle and lining fabric underskirts.

7) Stay-stitch front and back neck edges. Stitch side seams of bodice. Press open. Position the deepest part of the patchwork strip 35 mm (1$\frac{3}{8}$ in) from the lower edge of the bodice, back and front. Pin and tack, then fix with tiny invisible slip stitches. Press lightly.

8) Stitch the centre back seam of the skirt from the lower edge to the small dot. To reinforce the seam, back-stitch at the dot. Press seam open below the dot. Stitch skirt side seams. Press.

9) Position patchwork border around the skirt, with the deeper part of the pattern 7 cm (2⅔ in) away from the raw lower edge of the skirt. Pin and tack into place, then fix with invisible slip stitches. Press lightly. It is a good idea to neaten the seams as you go along. It is easier to do it gradually on such a small garment.

10) Pin the lining and the tulle underskirts at the waist, together with the skirt. (The tulle underskirt goes immediately under the dress fabric.) Run 2 lines of gathers round the waist and through all 3 'skirts' – by hand or on the machine to within 3 cm (1¼ in) of the opening at the back. Pull gathers to fit around the bodice.

11) With right sides together, pin skirt to bodice, matching centres and the side seams. Pin and tack gathers evenly on to the bodice. Machine-stitch. Press the seam towards the bodice. Avoid pressing over gathers. Machine-stitch the bodice shoulder seams. Press. Gather 40 cm (16 in) of lace, pin and tack to the neck edge, right sides together.

12) Assemble the bodice lining in the same way as the bodice itself. With right sides together, pin the lining to the bodice at the neck edge, matching centre fronts and the shoulder seams. Machine-stitch around the neck, making sure that the lace is not caught in the seam. Trim off excess cloth, clip all round the neck. (For advice on these operations, refer to dress-making instructions on page 138.)

13) Turn in the seam allowance along the back opening. Turn in the lining and slip-stitch in position. Continue this operation along the opening of the skirt. Turn in the bottom of the bodice lining and pin it over the gathers of the skirt, hiding the seam. Slip-stitch. In this way the 'wrong' side of the dress will be neat and all the seams hidden. It also reinforces this delicate garment.

14) Tack the lining and the dress fabric around the armholes. Gather the top of the sleeves, between outer dots. Stitch the underarm seams. Neaten and press. Gather the lower edge of the sleeves.

15) Stitch the cuff underarm seam and press open. Press under 1.5 cm (⅝ in) on one raw edge. Trim to 6 mm (¼ in). With right sides together, pin cuffs to sleeves,

matching underarm seams and large dots. Pull up gathers to fit. Pin and tack in position, adjusting gathers evenly. Machine-stitch. Trim the seam and fold the cuff. Slip-stitch pressed edge of cuff over the seam, matching underarm seams and large dots. Press.

16) Turn the sleeves right side out. Hold the dress, lining side out, with the armhole towards you. With right-hand sides together, pin the sleeve to the armhole edge with the small centre dot at the shoulder seam, matching underarm seams and remaining small dots. Machine-stitch and neaten seam.

17) Hemming the skirt. Turn up the raw edge by 3 cm (1¼ in) and press. Tack close to the pressed edge. Turn in the raw edge and pin, inserting the pins vertically and very close together as you will need to ease the fullness. Refer to instructions for this type of hem on page 141 and hand-hem neatly.

18) Trim the tulle underskirt to the same length as the finished skirt, then stitch the lace to the very edge, allowing the scallops to show. Hem the lining material underskirt a fraction shorter than the dress.

19) Make the buttonholes by hand or by machine, and stitch on buttons. Attach bows of narrow ribbon to the front of the bodice (refer to photographs of dress).

Overleaf you will find a detailed, half-size pattern in 3 sizes.

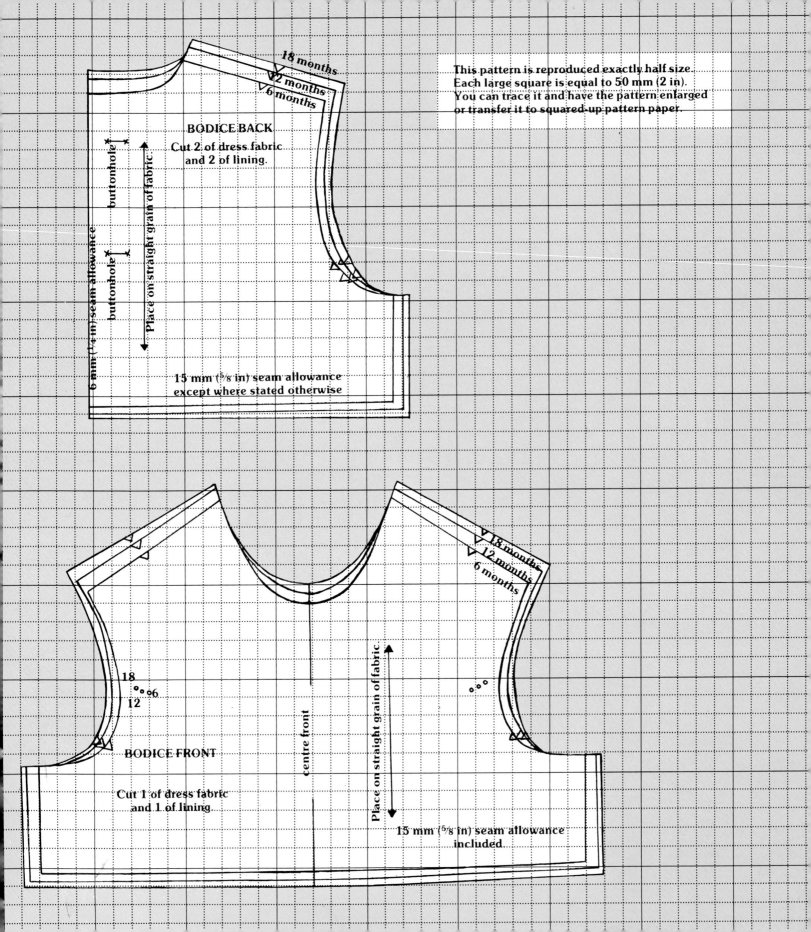

18 months
12 months
6 months

This pattern is reproduced exactly half size.
Each large square is equal to 50 mm (2 in).
You can trace it and have the pattern enlarged
or transfer it to squared-up pattern paper.

BODICE BACK
Cut 2 of dress fabric
and 2 of lining.

buttonhole
buttonhole
buttonhole

6 mm (¼ in) seam allowance

Place on straight grain of fabric

15 mm (⅝ in) seam allowance
except where stated otherwise

18 months
12 months
6 months

18
6
12

BODICE FRONT

centre front

Place on straight grain of fabric

Cut 1 of dress fabric
and 1 of lining

15 mm (⅝ in) seam allowance
included

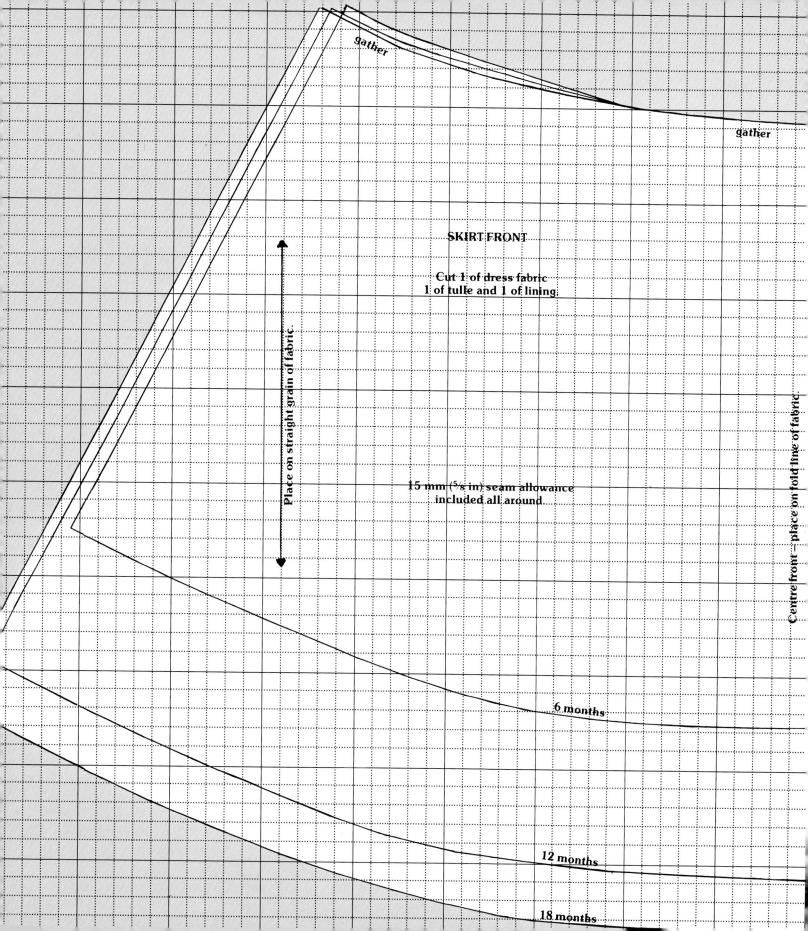

gather

gather

SKIRT FRONT

Cut 1 of dress fabric
1 of tulle and 1 of lining

Place on straight grain of fabric.

15 mm (⅝ in) seam allowance
included all around.

Centre front – place on fold line of fabric.

6 months

12 months

18 months

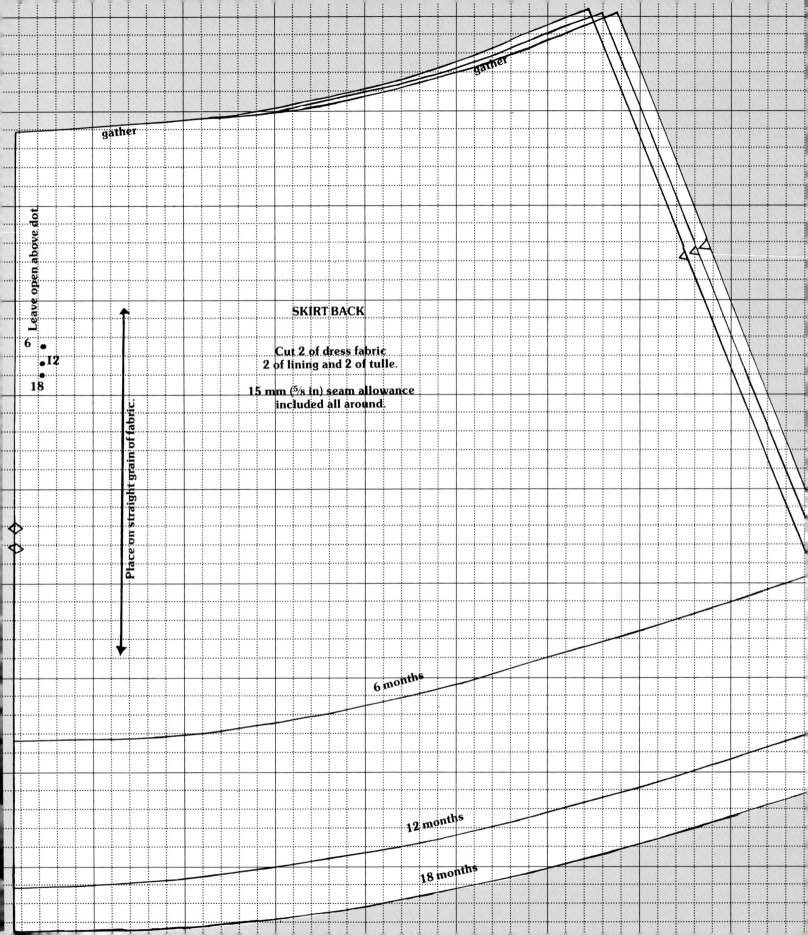

gather

gather

Leave open above dot

6
12
18

Place on straight grain of fabric.

SKIRT BACK

Cut 2 of dress fabric
2 of lining and 2 of tulle.

15 mm (⅝ in) seam allowance
included all around.

6 months

12 months

18 months

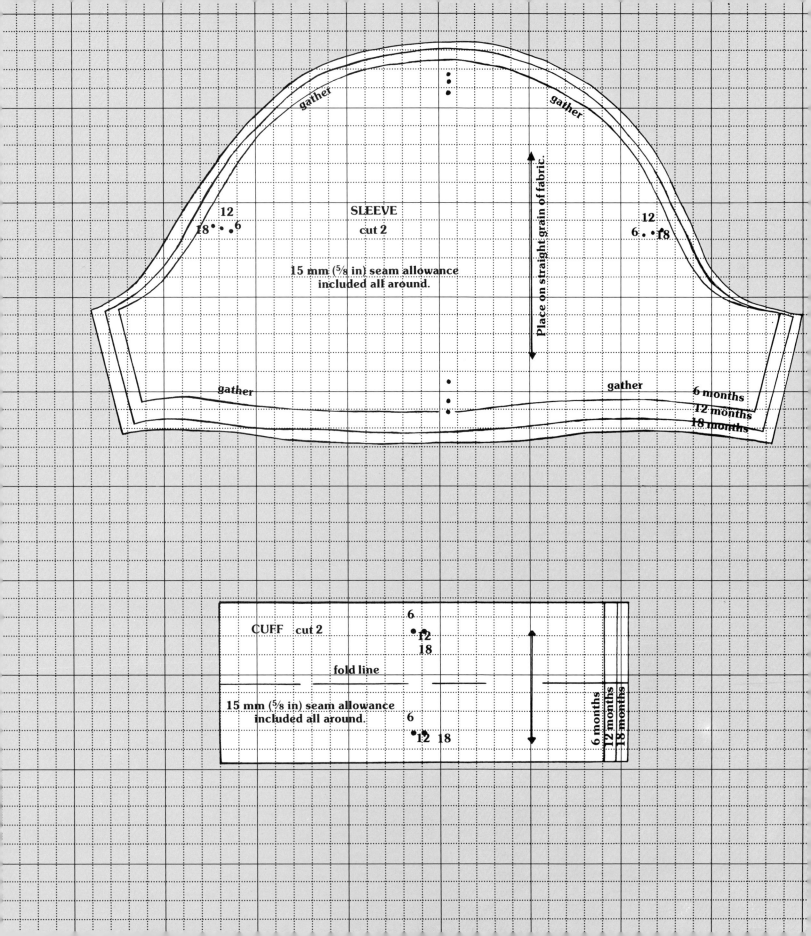

His First Party Rompers

This dainty romper suit matches the dress on page 8. Like the dress, it was worked in cream-coloured jacquard silk. The Dresden Plate border was worked in raw silks and fine Liberty prints.

YOU WILL NEED

Fabric: jacquard silk or raw silk, cotton lawn, cotton and polyester mix

Size **Fabric width:**		6 months	12 months	18 months
	115 cm	1.20 m	1.25 m	1.30 m
	45 in	1⅜ yd	1⅜ yd	1⅜ yd
	150 cm	0.85 m	0.85 m	0.85 m
	60 in	1 yd	1 yd	1 yd

N.B. These quantities allow enough fabric for lining the bodice of the romper suit.

Lightweight iron-on interfacing: 20 cm (8 in)

Matching thread

2 small plastic popper fasteners

8 small buttons

Stiff paper and cardboard for templates

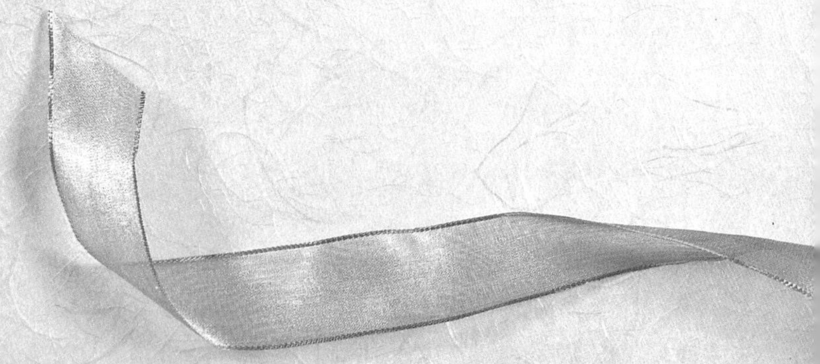

For the patchwork: 10 cm (4 in) of six different fabrics. I used raw silk for the 3 plain colours and printed cotton lawns for the rest.

This jacquard silk romper suit matches the dress on page 8. It would make a wonderful christening outfit.

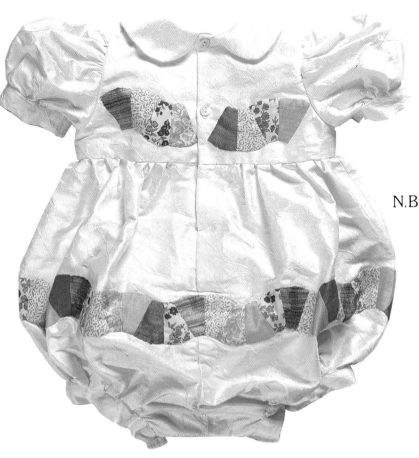

The back of the bodice has 2 buttons and the opening at the back of the trousers is fastened with 2 small poppers.

N.B. The patchwork seam allowance is 6 mm (¼ in).

1) Use the template and instructions 1) to 4) on pages 10 and 11 to cut 70 paper templates. Use 52 pieces to make up the border at the base of the rompers, 10 pieces for the front of the bodice and 4 pieces for each side of the back.

2) A detailed pattern of the rompers appears on pages 22 to 25. Referring to instructions 5) to 7) on page 11, cut out the pieces and make up the bodice. Attach the patchwork border.

3) The trousers. Stitch front centre seam. Run over the same seam again to reinforce it. Trim seam below notch to 6 mm (¼ in). Press seam open and neaten. To form the crotch, press attached facing along the fold line. Turn under 6 mm (¼ in) from the raw edge. Press and machine-stitch close to the edge. Repeat for the back of the trousers.

4) Join front and back of the trousers. Press seams flat and neaten. Attach the patchwork border (the highest curves of the pattern should be 132 mm (5½ in) away from the upper raw edge of the trousers. Gather base of trouser legs between the dots.

5) Gather the top of the trousers to within 3 cm (1¼ in) of back opening edges. With right sides together, pin trousers to bodice, matching centre and side seams. Pull gathers to fit and adjust them evenly. Pin, tack and machine-stitch. Press seam towards bodice. Avoid pressing over the gathers.

Above. *Detail from the patchwork border*

6) Fold one of the back facings along the centre fold line, right sides together. Stitch across each end, 1 cm (³⁄₈ in) away from raw edge. Clip corners. Turn right side out . Press. Make second facing in the same way.

7) Pin one of the facings to the right centre back of the trousers, with raw edges matching and the top edge of the facing level with the small dot. Stitch 1 cm (³⁄₈ in) away from the raw seam. Press facing flat under the edge of the trousers. Slip-stitch into place. Repeat with left centre back opening. Press facing away from trouser so that the two facings overlap each other. Oversew the lower edges of the facings together by hand and neaten the raw edge on the left-hand side.

8) Apply interfacing to one pair of collar sections. Pin right sides together – collar to collar facings – leaving the neck edge open. Layer seams and notch curves. Turn the collar right side out and press. Tack raw edges together and attach the 2 collar sections from underneath, matching dots. Clip neck edge of bodice to stay-stitching at curves. Tack collar – facings to neck edge – matching centre and shoulder dots.

9) Make up the bodice lining in the same way as the bodice. Pin lining to bodice at the neck edge, right sides together and over collar, matching dots. Stitch edges of the back of the bodice and around the neck with a continuous seam, 1 cm (³⁄₈ in) wide. Clip curves.

10) Turn the lining right side out. Press. Slip-stitch the bottom edge over the gathers around the waist. Set in the sleeves, following instructions 14) to 16) to the matching dress on pages 12 and 13.

11) Press under 1.5 cm (⁵⁄₈ in) along one long edge of leg cuff. Trim to 6 mm (¹⁄₄ in). Fold the cuff along fold line. Stitch across ends. Trim seams. Turn the cuff right side out. Press. Pin the right side of the cuff to the wrong side of the romper leg, matching dots. Pull up gathering stitches to fit and finish off in the same way as the sleeve cuff. Repeat for the other leg. Work 6 buttonholes along the front of the crotch and 2 at the back of the bodice. Stitch the buttons. Attach the poppers.

Overleaf. *The pattern is reproduced exactly half size. Each large square is equal to 50 mm (2 in). You can trace it and have the pattern enlarged or transfer it to squared-up pattern paper.*

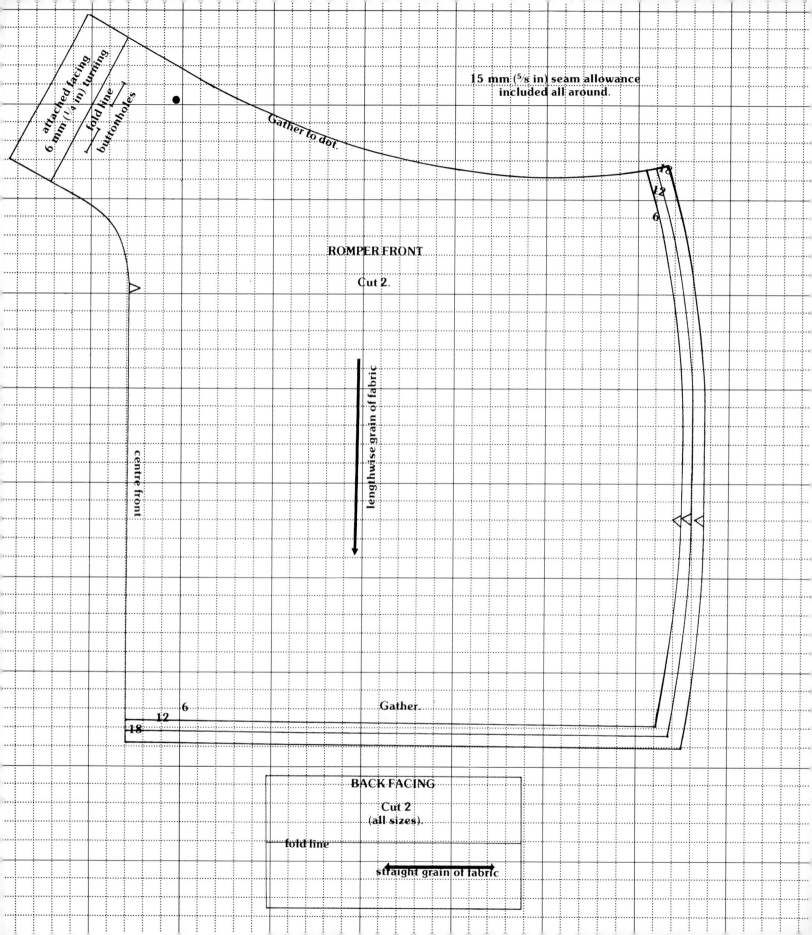

15 mm (⅝ in) seam allowance
included all around.

attached facing
6 mm (¼ in) turning

fold line

buttonholes

Gather to dot.

18
12
6

ROMPER FRONT

Cut 2.

lengthwise grain of fabric

centre front

6
12
18

Gather

BACK FACING

Cut 2
(all sizes).

fold line

straight grain of fabric

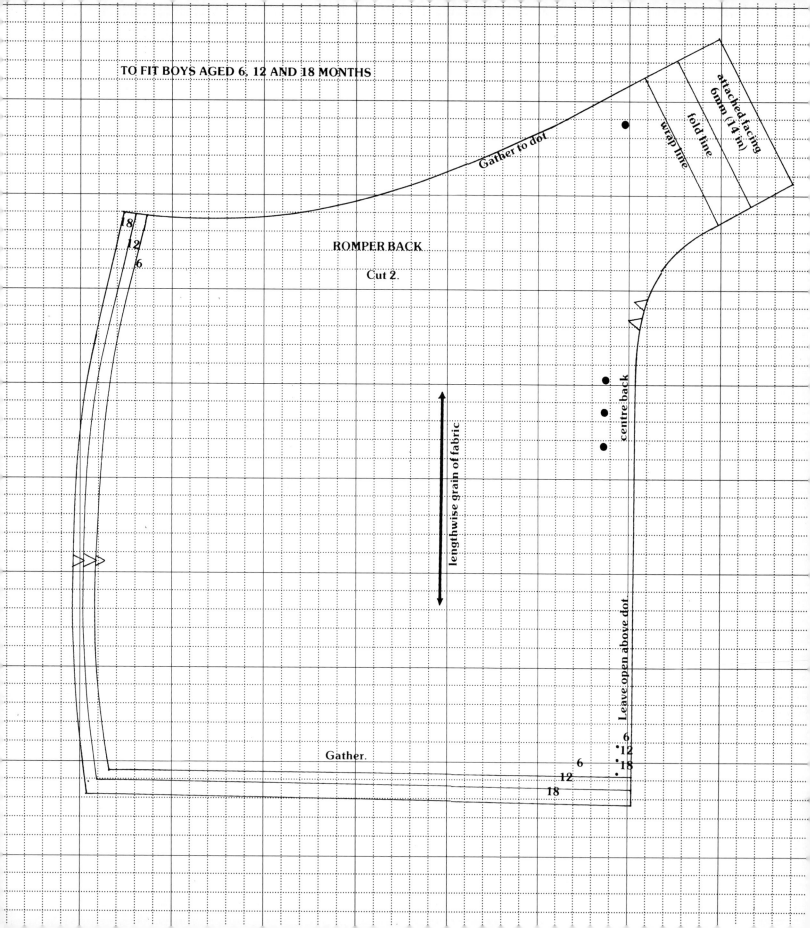

TO FIT BOYS AGED 6, 12 AND 18 MONTHS

ROMPER BACK

Cut 2.

attached facing
6mm (¼ in)

fold line

wrap line

Gather to dot

18
12
6

lengthwise grain of fabric

centre back

Leave open above dot

Gather.

6
12
18

6
12
18

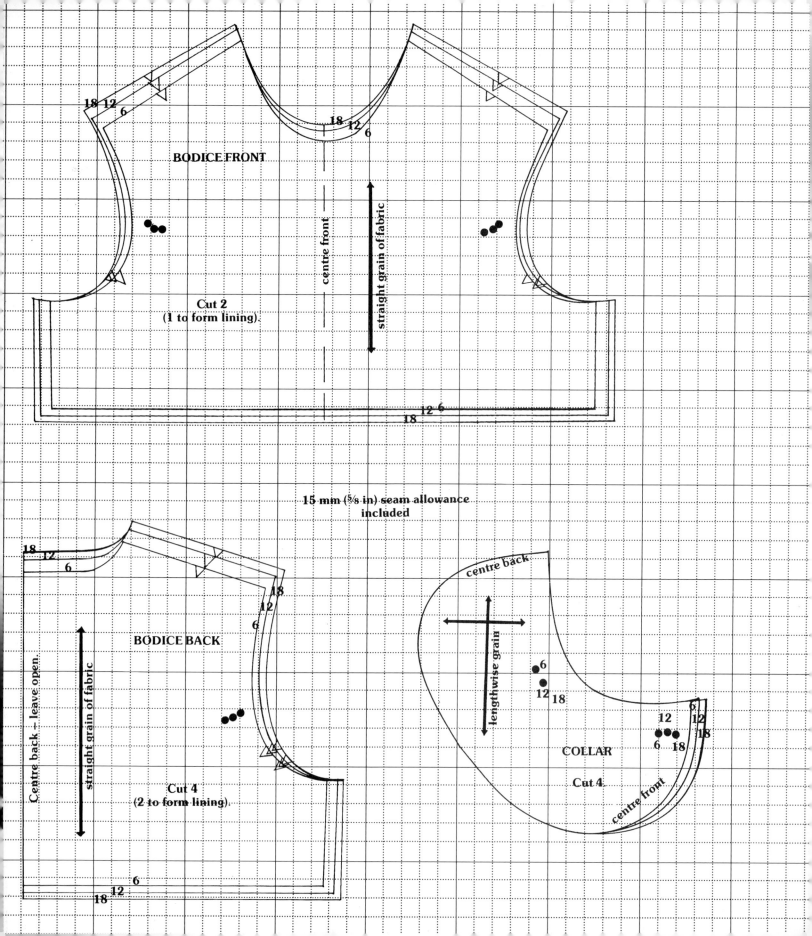

BODICE FRONT

18 12
6

18 12
6

centre front

straight grain of fabric

Cut 2
(1 to form lining)

18 12 6

15 mm (⅜ in) seam allowance
included

18 12
6

BODICE BACK

18
12
6

Centre back – leave open.

straight grain of fabric

Cut 4
(2 to form lining)

6
18 12

centre back

lengthwise grain

6
12 18

COLLAR

Cut 4

12 6 12
6 18 18

centre front

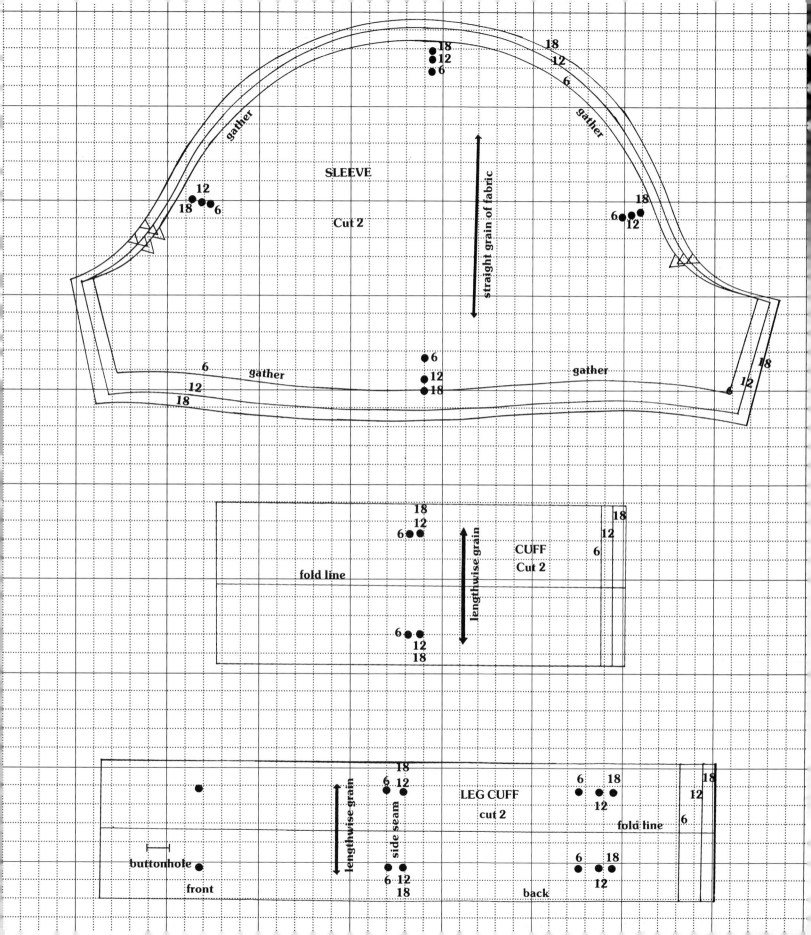

Sleepy-cat Quilt

T his cot quilt forms part of a range of nursery accessories which includes a matching cot bumper, a nursery organizer and a nappy holder. The fabric requirements are given for the individual projects, but if you wish to make all four items you will need 2.10 m (3 yd) of plain sheeting and 1.10 m (1½ yd) of polka-dot sheeting in the specified width of 228 cm (90 in). It is difficult to give exact quantities for the patchwork fabrics. As a guideline, I used approximately 90 cm (1 yd) of the floral fabric for the corner pieces of the quilt, etc. You will probably need the same quantity of your chosen fabric to do the cats' bodies, but ¼ m (10 in) of the other seven fabrics should be ample.

The Sleepy-cat Quilt measures 106 × 74 cm (42 × 29 in).

YOU WILL NEED

For the quilt:

Main colour fabric: 1.30 m (1½ yd) of plain polycotton sheeting 228 cm (90 in) wide.

Floral corner fabric: 40 cm (½ yd) in 90 cm (36 in) width

Cat's body: 30 cm (12 in)

Medium-weight polyester wadding: 1.15 m (1¼ yd) in 96 cm (38 in) width

Butter muslin: 1.15 m (1¼ yd) in 90 cm (36 in) width

Narrow ribbon: 1.75 m (2 yd)   Washable fabric marker

Toning thread   Black or dark brown stranded embroidery cotton for cat's features

Paper-backed fusible web

Cardboard for templates

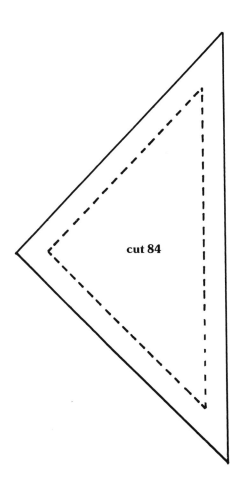

cut 84

For the patchwork: 20 cm (8 in) each of 7 contrasting/toning fabrics (polyester cotton, brushed cotton, cotton lawn)

N.B. All seam allowances, including patchwork, are 6 mm (¼ in).

1) Before cutting the quilt, it is advisable to assemble the patchwork border. The border consists of 84 triangles. In addition it has 4 small squares as corner pieces and 4 large squares for the corners of the quilt. Prepare cardboard templates from the patterns opposite. Cut all the triangles and the 2 sets of squares, using the templates provided. The border is made up of 26 triangles along the long dimension and 16 across the width. Arrange the triangles in position on a table top so that you can mix the colours in a pleasing manner. In this quilt I alternated light and dark triangles regularly in the border. Assemble the border using the American Seamed Patchwork technique; detailed instructions can be found on page 129.

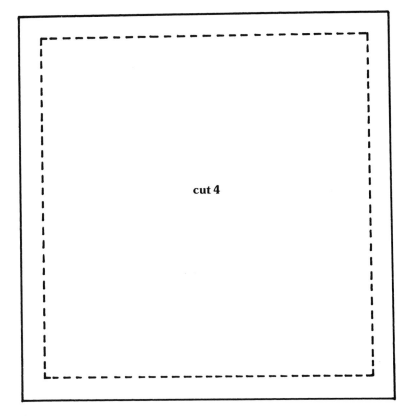

cut 4

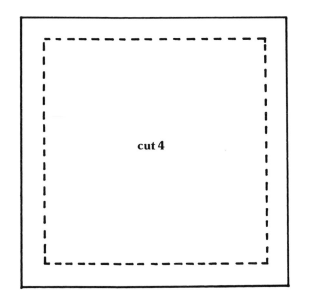

cut 4

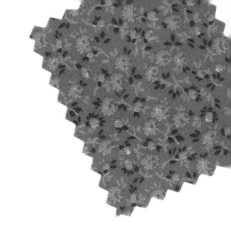

2) Make up the 2 long strips and the 2 short strips of triangles. The seam allowance for the patchwork is 6 mm (¼ in). It is important to sew accurately or the patchwork strips will come out different lengths.

3) Press the lengths of patchwork. The seams joining 2 patches must be pressed to one side (not opened) and pushed under the darker of the 2 patches. Measure the strips accurately and cut an oblong of the plain fabric the same size. This will form the top of the quilt.

4) Pin and machine-stitch the two long strips of patchwork along the rectangle. Fold the edge of the patchwork **under** the border to avoid see-through on the light-coloured quilt top, and press.

5) Machine-stitch the 4 small corner squares to the ends of the 2 shorter strips of patchwork. Press. Pin and

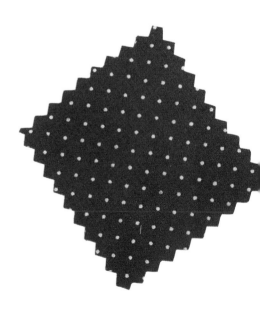

machine-stitch the 2 strips to the quilt top. Press the edges under the border as before.

6) Cutting and setting the outer border. The top of the quilt has a border made of the plain fabric and inset corners made of the floral material. Measure the outer length of the longer and shorter dimensions of the patchwork border, and add the width of the large corner squares you have already cut. Out of the plain material, cut 2 long and 2 short pieces according to these measurements. With right sides together, pin and machine-stitch the long strips to the quilt. Press the seams under the patchwork border.

7) Machine-stitch the 4 large corner squares to the ends of the 2 short strips. Press. Pin and machine-stitch these 2 panels as previously instructed. Press seams under patchwork.

8) Cut the back of the quilt out of plain material, to exactly the same measurements as the front. Keep to one side.

9) For the central cat motif, make cardboard templates using the patterns on page 32. (Enlarge them as directed.) Trace the pieces which form the cat and his cushion on to the paper side of the fusible web. Cut out, leaving at least a 6 mm (¼ in) allowance around each piece. Iron the shapes on to the cloth. Cut out the shapes accurately along the drawn lines and peel off the paper backing.

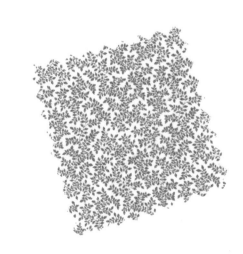

10) Position shapes, adhesive side down, on to the right side of the centre section of the quilt top. When you are entirely happy with the arrangement, start pressing the pieces into position. Trace the cat's features with the fabric marker and hand-embroider in stem stitch or backstitch.

11) Quilting. Lay the length of muslin flat on the table. Cover it with the wadding and finally lay the prepared quilt top – right side up – over it. Cut the muslin and wadding 12 mm (½ in) larger all round than the quilt top.

12) Smooth out from the centre, pinning all 3 layers together. Tack following instructions for quilting on page 136. Using the satin-stitch setting on your sewing machine, embroider around the cat and cushion pieces, ensuring that all the raw edges are covered.

A corner from the Sleepy-cat Quilt. The border and the floral corner pieces have been quilted 'in the ditch'. The instructions for this technique are found on page 136.

13) Using a machine straight stitch, medium length, quilt along both sides of the patchwork border and the corner squares. Sew 'in the ditch', that is in the very crease of the seam, so that the stitches almost disappear when the quilting is finished. Trim the wadding and muslin to the same size as the quilt top.

14) Lay the prepared quilt, cat side up, on the table. Overlay with the plain backing which you have already cut. Pin and tack. Machine-stitch around the outer edge, leaving a 30 cm (12 in) opening to enable you to turn the quilt inside out. Trim corners.

15) Turn quilt over and slip-stitch edges of the opening together. Trim with ribbon bows, stitched right through the knot so that the baby cannot tear them off.

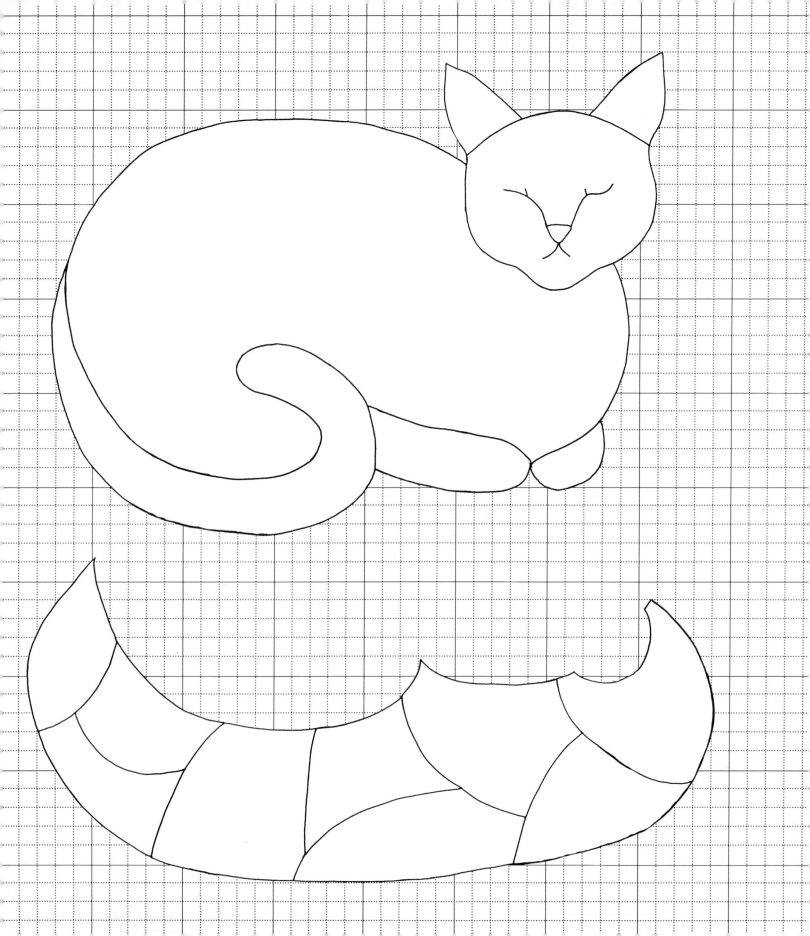

The cat and its cushion. To enlarge these patterns, refer to No. 5 on page 11.

Alexander, aged 6 months, sits on the Sleepy-cat Quilt while wearing one of the Seminole jackets (see page 80).

Cot Bumper

YOU WILL NEED

Main colour fabric: 50 cm (20 in) of polycotton sheeting 228 cm (90 in) wide

Polka-dot fabric: 50 cm (20 in) of polycotton sheeting, 228 cm (90 in) wide

Medium-weight polyester wadding: 1.80 m (2 yd), 96 cm (38 in) width

Butter muslin: 1.80 m (2 yd), 90 cm (36 in) wide

Toning thread   Thin cardboard

Paper-backed fusible web   Non-slip ribbon (optional)

Black or dark brown stranded embroidery thread for cat's features

The vertical lines of stitching should be positioned according to the width of the cot.

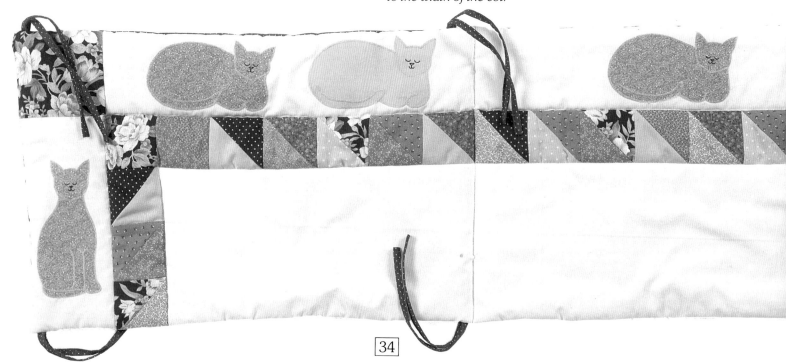

34

For the patchwork: 25 cm (10 in) each of 7 different cotton prints in light and dark tones

N.B. All seam allowances, including patchwork, are 6 mm (¼ in).

1) Using the template provided for the Sleepy-cat Quilt on page 28, cut 60 triangles and arrange them to achieve a pleasing mixture of colours. Here again, I have alternated light and dark fabrics. Cut 2 small and 2 large squares of floral fabric using the templates given at the bottom of page 28.

2) As instructed for the Quilt, make 1 long strip of 48 triangles and 2 short strips of 6 triangles each. Press as instructed previously. Use the measurements of the strips to cut the piece of plain material which forms the main part of the bumper. Assemble as in No. 3 of the Quilt (page 29). Join the small floral squares to one end of each short strip. Press. Pin and machine-stitch the short strips to the sides of the bumper. Cut and assemble the plain fabric border as explained in No. 6 of the Quilt.

The cat shapes on the left and on page 37 are shown real size. You will need 6 sitting cats and 2 upright ones. The design needs to be reversed so that all the cats look towards the centre of the bumper. This can be done using tracing paper. Some photocopiers can reverse a design.

3) Appliquéd cats. Using the patterns provided, cut out cardboard templates and use these to transfer the cat shapes on to the backing of the fusible web material. Apply as in No. 9 and 10 of the Quilt instructions.

4) Cut the back of the bumper out of the polka-dot material to the same size as the top of the bumper. Keep to one side.

5) Proceed as per No. 11 to 13 inclusive of the Quilt instructions.

6) Using offcuts of the polka-dot fabric, cut 4 pairs of ties 40 cm (16 in) long and 25 mm (1 in) wide. These will enable you to fix the bumper to the cot (see No. 7 below). Alternatively, use lengths of non-slip ribbon. Position the ties on the prepared bumper and pin in place. (Refer to the photograph for guidance.)

7) The width of cots is far from standard. Look at the photograph of the bumper on pages 34–35 and you will see that there are 2 vertical lines of stitches which go right through the finished quilting. These are spaced according to the width of the cot. (This dimension also affects the position of the ties.) To ensure that you stitch accurately, draw both lines using a washable fabric marker. (Do *not* machine-stitch them yet.)

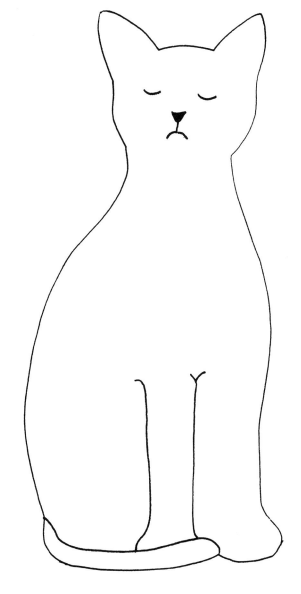

8) Proceed as per No. 14 and 15 of the Quilt. Finally, work the 2 lines of stitching which you have traced as per instructions in No. 7 above.

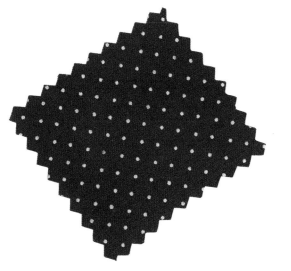

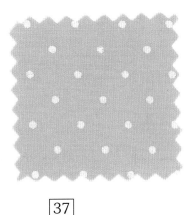

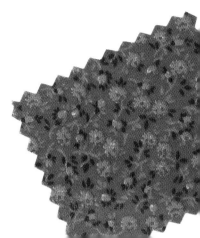

Nursery Organizer

This handy multi-pocketed organizer has been designed to hang from a cot. It will keep all of baby's toiletries close at hand. It is quick and easy to make – the perfect present!

YOU WILL NEED

Main colour fabric: 60 cm (¾ yd) of plain polycotton sheeting, 228 cm (90 in) wide

Polka-dot fabric: 60 cm (¾ yd) of polycotton sheeting, 228 cm (90 in) wide

Floral corner fabric: 25 cm (10 in)

Heavy-weight sew-in interfacing: 60 cm (¾ yd) in 96 cm (38 in) width

Narrow elastic: 30 cm (12 in)

Paper-backed fusible web

Narrow ribbon: 50 cm (20 in)

Cardboard for templates

Non-slip ribbon (optional)

Toning thread

Small strip of adhesive Velcro tape or 2 plastic poppers (optional)

For the patchwork: 10 cm (4 in) each of 8 different printed fabrics (includes cats)

N.B. All seam allowances, including patchwork, are 6 mm (¼ in).

1) Using the template provided for the Quilt on page 28, cut 14 triangles out of the printed fabric. Use the small square template at the bottom left of page 28 to cut 4 pieces of floral material and 2 of your main fabric material.

The finished nursery organizer, ready to be hung from baby's cot. Its size is approximately 56 × 65 cm (22 × 25½ in).

2) Arrange the triangles to your satisfaction and make up the strip of patchwork as instructed for the Quilt. Join one floral square at either end of the patchwork strip. Press as instructed for the Quilt.

3) Measure the finished strip and use this dimension to cut the strip of plain fabric which fits above the patchwork. The width of this strip is the same as that of the floral squares. Join the remaining 2 floral squares at either end of the plain fabric. Join the 2 plain squares at either end of the patchwork strip. Pin with right sides together and machine-stitch along the length of the 2 strips. Press flat, folding the seam **under** the patchwork border to avoid see-through.

4) Now cut the front part of the organizer out of your main fabric. Check the width of the patchwork panel – *approximately* 67 cm (26½ in). Use this as the long dimension and cut a rectangle 47 cm (18½ in) deep. Join it on to the patchwork panel. Press.

The detail above shows the pleat formed on either side of the bottom pockets and the Velcro fastenings under the flap of the middle pocket.

5) Lay the interfacing on the table. Place the front of the organizer right side up on top. Pin and cut the interfacing to size. Tack together.

6) Out of the polka-dot material cut an oblong to the same size as the front of the organizer. Keep to one side.

7) The bottom pockets are made up of 4 pieces each measuring 25 cm (10 in) square, including a 6 mm (¼ in) seam allowance. Cut them out of the 3 different fabrics (refer to photograph on page 39) and join them together to make a strip.

8) Use the patterns given for the Cot Bumper on pages 36–37 to cut out all 3 cat shapes. Apply as in No. 9 and 10 of the Quilt instructions. Fix the 2 upright cats on the light-coloured pockets. Using the satin-stitch setting on the machine, go round the shapes to ensure that no raw edges show through. Embroider the cats' features by hand, using stem stitch and back stitch.

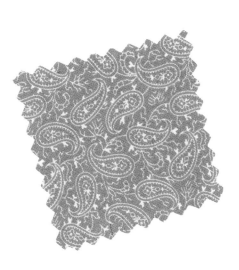

9) Lining the pockets. Lay the light-coloured fabric on the table, right side up. Put the strip you have made for the pockets right side down over it, pin and cut. Machine-stitch all round, leaving a 15 cm (6 in) opening at the base of the pockets for turning over. Clip the corners. Turn the piece inside out. Press flat, including the turnings along the opening, then pin these shut. Run a line of top-stitching close to the top edge of the pockets to reinforce them.

10) To position the bottom pockets on the front panel of the organizer, find the centre point at the base of the panel and mark it with a pin. The pockets are attached 12 mm (½ in) from the bottom and side edges of the front panel. If you think of the centre of the panel as the dividing line between pockets 2 and 3, find the centre of each side and mark the division between pockets 1 and 2, and 3 and 4 with a pin. Using a washable fabric marker, draw vertical lines up from each marker pin to guide you when you come to attach the pockets to the front panel. Pin the pockets over these lines, 12 mm (½ in) from the bottom.

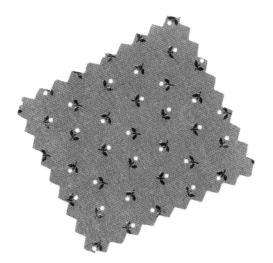

11) Starting from the left, pin and machine-stitch the left-hand side of the floral pocket on to the panel – 12 mm (½ in) away from the bottom and left edges as explained before. Run a vertical line of stitching along the other pocket divides you have pinned. Pin and machine-stitch the right-hand side of the fourth pocket 12 mm (½ in) from the bottom and outer edge of the front panel.

12) Base of pockets. Make a pleat at either side of each pocket so that the fabric lies flat and does not go over the dividing lines between the pockets (refer to photograph on page 40). Pin into position and repeat this process for all 4 pockets. Run one line of top-stitching close to the edge of the pockets and a second line 6 mm (¼ in) above it.

13) Top pockets. The polka-dot pocket and the floral one are made of a single thickness of fabric, measuring 140 × 115 mm (5½ × 4½ in) and 190 × 210 mm (7½ × 8¼ in) respectively. Cut them out. Run a line of zig-zag stitches along the top of the pockets to prevent fraying. Measure 25 mm (1 in) from the top of the pockets, fold over (wrong sides together) and press.

14) Run a line of stitching 12 mm (½ in) from the top of both pockets, then a second line 6 mm (¼ in) further down. This will form a channel for the elastic.

15) Polka-dot pocket. Run a piece of elastic 75 mm (3 in) long through the channel. Anchor firmly at either end. Repeat the process for the floral pocket with a piece of elastic measuring 140 mm (5½ in) long. Turning the raw edges of the pockets over 6 mm (¼ in), press flat. Keep to one side.

16) Centre pocket. Cut 2 pieces out of the light-coloured fabric, each measuring 380 × 150 mm (15 × 6 in) inclusive of seam allowance. Iron on the cat shape, go round with satin stitch and hand-embroider the face as explained in No. 7 above. Position this pocket 180 mm (7 in) from the left-hand edge of the front panel and 170 mm (6¾ in) from the top, and mount to the front panel in the same way as the bottom pockets. Run a vertical line of stitching along the left-hand side of the pocket. Attach the right-hand side of the pocket 255 mm (10 in) away from the right-hand edge of the panel. Make 2 pleats on either side of the pocket so that it lies flat. Pin into position and finish off with 2 lines of top-stitching at the base of the pocket, as you did for the bottom pockets.

17) The pocket flap is made of a double thickness of fabric which is the length of the finished pocket, adding 12 mm (½ in) seam allowance. The depth of the flap is 55 mm (2¼ in) inclusive of seam allowance. Stitch all round the flap, leaving a small gap. Turn the piece inside out and press flat. Pin the top of the flap above the pocket and 150 mm (6 in) from the top of the front panel. Run one line of top-stitching very close to the top edge of the flap and a second line 6 mm (¼ in) further down. Attach 2 small pieces of

adhesive Velcro or poppers to the inside of the flap and to the front of the pocket if desired.

18) Position polka-dot and floral pockets on either side of the central pocket. They should be laid flat – not stretching the elastic – as you can see in the photograph. Pin and run one line of top-stitching close to the edges. The front panel of the organizer is now complete.

19) With the front panel right side up on the table, lay the polka-dot backing over it so that the right sides are together. Make five or six pairs of ties or use lengths of non-slip ribbon, as explained in No. 6 of the Cot Bumper instructions. Position them according to the design of the cot.

20) Stitch all round the organizer, 6 mm (¼ in) from the edge, leaving a 30 cm (12 in) gap at the top of the panel. Trim the edges of the interfacing close to the seam, clip the corners and turn the piece inside out. Press. Pin open edges together. Run a line of top-stitching close to the edge of the entire piece. You can also top-stitch along the edges of the patchwork border and the corner squares to strengthen the top of the panel. Trim with ribbon bows.

On the following pages you will find the instructions for the Nappy-holder which completes this range of nursery accessories.

Nappy-holder

YOU WILL NEED

Main colour fabric: 50 cm (20 in) polycotton sheeting, 228 cm (90 in) wide

Polka-dot fabric: 60 cm (¾ yd) polycotton sheeting, 228 cm (90 in) wide

A piece of hardboard cut to 38 × 28 cm (15 × 11 in) for the base

Narrow ribbon   Toning thread   Stranded embroidery cotton

Paper-backed fusible web   Cardboard for templates

Child-size wooden coat hanger   PVA adhesive

Short length of cream-coloured bias binding to cover hook

For the patchwork: 10 cm (4 in) each of 8 different cotton prints (inclusive of floral material)

N.B. All seam allowances, including patchwork, are 6 mm (¼ in).

1) The working method is the same as for the other pieces in this collection. Refer to No. 1 and 2 of the Quilt instructions. Cut 52 triangles, using the template shown on page 28. You will also need 6 of the small floral corner pieces, cut using the template at the bottom left of page 28. Make the long strip first, using 32 triangles, then the two short ones with 10 triangles on either side.

2) Measure the long and one of the short strips and use these measurements to cut an oblong of light-coloured fabric which will form the main part of the holder.

3) Attach a floral square at either end of each short strip. Press. As before, pin and machine-stitch the long strip of patchwork to the edge of the rectangle of light-coloured fabric, right sides together. Pin and machine-stitch the 2 short lengths of patchwork to the shorter dimensions of the rectangle. Press, pushing the seams under border.

Right. *The finished nappy-holder with a wide-awake cat lurking inside.*

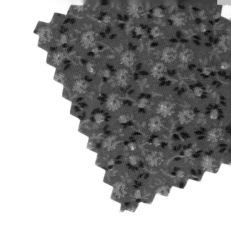

4) Cut the 3 strips of light-coloured fabric to fit along the patchwork border. These strips should be the same width as the floral squares. Pin and machine-stitch the longer strip along the bottom edge of the patchwork border. Pin and machine-stitch the 2 remaining floral squares at one end of each short plain strip. Join these to the short sides of the patchwork with the floral squares at the bottom (refer to photograph). Press as before.

5) Cut an oblong of polka-dot material to form the lining of the holder, exactly the same size as the top panel.

6) Enlarge the pattern on page 47, make a template out of cardboard and use it to trace the tall cat shape out of fusible web material. Position the cat at the centre of the piece of polka-dot lining. Make sure the cat is positioned accurately so that it can be seen through the front opening of the holder. Iron into place.

7) Go round the cat shape with satin stitch as explained for the other pieces. Hand-embroider the cat's face.

8) Lay the prepared panel with the patchwork face up on the table. Place the lining with the appliquéd cat face down over it. (Make sure the cat is pointing upwards.) Run a line of stitches along the 2 short dimensions. Turn the piece inside out. Press flat. Run a line of top-stitching close to the edge of the stitched sides which will form the front opening of the holder. Pin and machine-stitch the top and bottom of the panel to hold the 2 layers of fabric together.

9) Flat base of holder. Out of the light-coloured fabric, cut an oblong 392 × 292 mm (15¼ × 11½ in). Mark the centre of one of the long dimensions with a pin. Find the centre of the bottom edge of the patchwork panel and mark this with a pin too. Align the 2 pins. Pin the panel all round. If you have measured correctly, the gap at the front of the holder should be centred. Adjust if necessary. Machine-stitch and neaten the seam, including the edge along the front opening. Press down.

10) Using the pre-cut piece of hardboard as a template, cut a piece of polka-dot material, allowing 25 mm (1 in) all round for turning over. Fix the edges of the cloth over the board with glue. Allow to dry.

11) The exact shape and width of the top of the holder is determined by the size of your coat hanger. Make yourself a paper pattern, the top should slope or curve according to the shape of the hanger. Lay the pattern over the folded material to obtain 2 shapes, not forgetting a generous seam allowance. The front of this top panel should be at least 115 mm (4½ in) deep from the base of the hook to accommodate the appliquéd cat. Cut out the latter, using the template opposite. Iron on and embroider as before.

12) Stitch along the curved top of the panel, leaving a tiny gap in the centre to fit over the hook of the hanger. Turn inside out and trim seams if necessary. Press seams. Make a 6 mm (¼ in) turnover along the raw edges. Press.

13) Use the bias binding to cover the hook. Starting at the open end of the hook, hold the end of the bias a little way along the hook and wind the bias tightly over and around to cover the end and make sure it cannot come undone. Secure the end with a few stitches when you reach the hanger. Cover the hanger by winding strips of the light-coloured fabric around it.

14) Slip the shaped panel over the coat hanger with the small cat facing you. Mark the centre of the back of this panel with a pin. Find and mark with a pin the centre of the top of the patchwork panel. Align the 2 pins.

15) Moving to the front of the top panel, mark with pins an area of approximately 75 mm (3 in) which will form the front opening – centre it accurately under the cat. On either side of the patchwork panel, form 2 deep pleats of equal depth to reduce the fullness at the top of the holder so that it will fit the width of the shaped top panel. Pin and machine-stitch the top edge to hold the pleats.

16) Tack the top panel over this seam with the coat hanger in position. Make sure that the front and back of the top panel align. Top-stitch close to the edge and run a second line of stitching 6 mm (¼ in) above the first. Fix a small bow under the cat's chin and one at the base of the hook. Slide in the detachable hardboard base.

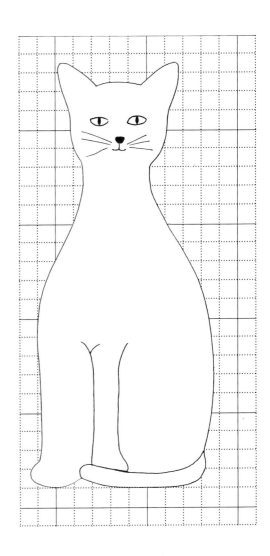

This cat shape is shown half size. Enlarge as per No. 5 on page 11.

Baby's Best Bib

These colourful bibs make small but very special presents. They are also perfect projects on which to experiment with an unfamiliar patchwork technique. For the Log Cabin variation bib, refer to general instructions on page 130; for the pin-wheel star bib look up the American Seamed Patchwork technique on page 129; the English tumbling block pattern is constructed like English Patchwork: see page 128; and the technique used for the Crazy Patchwork bib is explained on page 131.

YOU WILL NEED

For each bib:

Terry towelling: 1 33 cm (13 in) square

Toning or contrasting bias: 1.50 m (59 in)

Crazy Patchwork and Log Cabin bibs:

Cotton lawn to use as base:

1 33 cm (13 in) square for each bib

Matching thread

For the patchwork: For the pin-wheel star bib you will need 4 co-ordinating pieces of cotton 23 cm (9 in) square.
For the other bibs you will need an assortment of scraps of washable lightweight cotton prints.

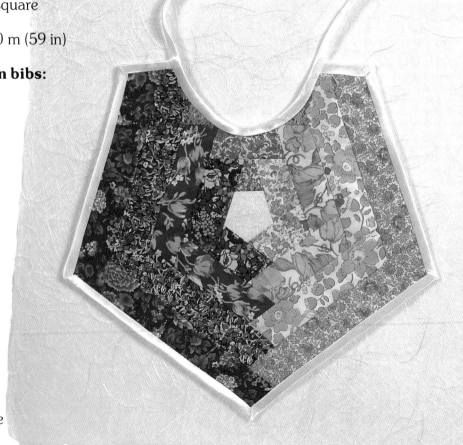

Log-cabin variation bib

English tumbling blocks

Pin-wheel star bib

Crazy patchwork bib

N.B. All seam allowances including patchwork are 6 mm (¼ in).

Log Cabin variation bib. Enlarge the pattern together with the pentagonal template on page 53 and use these to mark the white fabric base and to cut the pentagonal piece which forms the centre of the pattern. The technique followed is exactly the same as that described on page 130, except that the centre piece is pentagonal rather than square. Using the template on page 52, cut the strips in a colour range of your choice.

The pin-wheel star bib. Using the square and triangular templates provided on page 52 and following the instructions for American Seamed Patchwork on page 129, construct the block, joining the pieces in the order shown in the diagram on the right. The pattern works best if fabrics of contrasting tones are used. When the block is complete, sew a 5 cm (2 in) wide strip of one of the fabrics used to each side of the block. Press seams. You now have a square of 'fabric' large enough to cut out the bib.

English tumbling blocks bib. Using the inner part of the diamond-shaped template shown on the opposite page, make a master and cut 56 paper templates. Sort out your fabrics into light, medium and dark tones. Using the outer part of the template, make a master and cut 18 light diamonds, 19 medium and 19 dark. Arrange them in rows so that the dark, light and mid-toned pieces all face the same way to give the three-dimensional 'block' effect. See sketch opposite.

This is the order in which the pin-wheel is assembled. Make up one strip as shown, then the other two. Finally, join all three strips together.

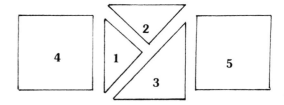

This sketch shows how to alternate light, mid and dark tones to create the 'tumbling-block' effect.

All four bibs are lined with terry towelling.

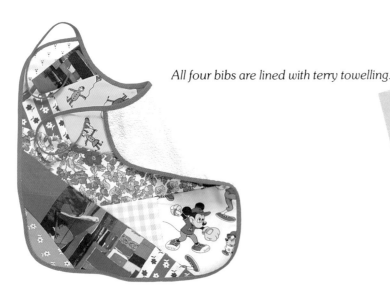

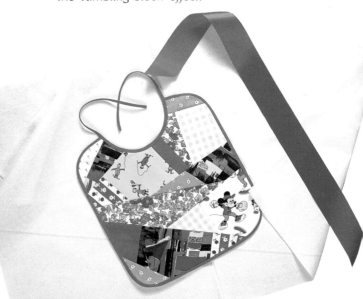

Following the instructions for English Patchwork on page 128, make up a piece of patchwork measuring approximately 30.5 cm (12 in) square.

Crazy Patchwork bib. Following the instructions on page 131 and using the piece of white cotton as a base, make up a piece of patchwork 30.5 cm (12 in) square.

1) Making up the bibs. Press the patchwork pieces and, in the case of the tumbling block bib, remove the tacking and the paper templates. If you are making the pin-wheel star, the tumbling blocks or the Crazy Patchwork bib, enlarge the pattern given on top of page 53 and use it to cut out the bib – the Log Cabin variation has its own pattern which you should already have enlarged or traced to produce the cotton base for the patchwork.

2) Make sure you place the pattern centrally over the patchwork. Cut out the patchwork and lay it over the towelling material (wrong sides together). Cut out the backing to the same size as the patchwork. Tack the two layers together.

3) Bind the outer edge of the bibs with bias binding, cutting the ends of the tape flush with the neck edge. Bind the neck edge, leaving approximately 20 cm (8 in) on either side for the ties. (Refer to the dress-making section on page 140). Slip-stitch the edges of the bias tape together to form the ties.

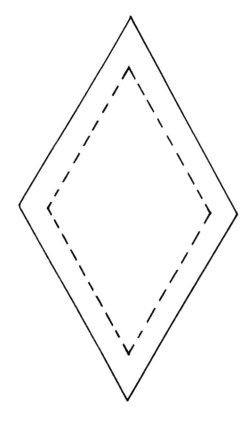

Use the inner part of this pattern to cut the paper templates. You will need 56 of these. Use the outer template to cut the fabric pieces.

Quite different in style, these bibs will make welcome gifts.

These 3 templates are used to produce the pin-wheel star design.

Use this template to cut the strips of fabric for the Log Cabin variation bib.

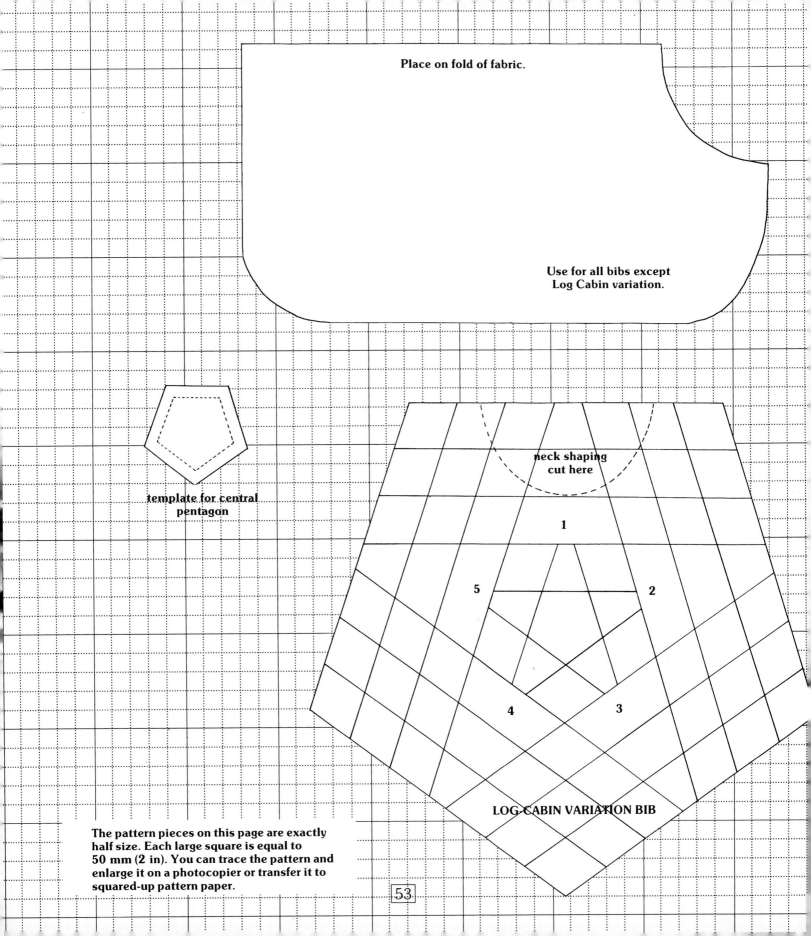

Place on fold of fabric.

Use for all bibs except
Log Cabin variation.

template for central
pentagon

neck shaping
cut here

1

5   2

4   3

LOG CABIN VARIATION BIB

The pattern pieces on this page are exactly
half size. Each large square is equal to
50 mm (2 in). You can trace the pattern and
enlarge it on a photocopier or transfer it to
squared-up pattern paper.

The finished range of accessories. The floppy cushion measures approximately 58 cm (23 in) square.

Nursery Accessories

This range of objects, consisting of a large floppy cushion to fit in a nursing chair, a toiletry basket, a pincushion and a small bag for cotton wool, is made in English Patchwork. The cool, fresh colours contribute to the charm of this collection.

YOU WILL NEED

For the cushion:

White fabric: 1 piece 51 cm (20 in) square of polycotton, lawn or other material (front of cushion)

1 piece 51 × 63 cm (20 × 25 in) (back of cushion)

1 strip 4.5 m × 125 mm (5 yd × 5 in) (for the frill). The material can be joined

Cushion pad: 45 cm (18 in) square

Narrow lace: 2m (2¼ yd)

Ribbon: 1 m (1¼ yd), 25 mm (1 in) wide

Buttons, popper fasteners or Velcro tape for fastening (optional)

White thread

Toning thread for the patchwork

Stiff paper for templates and cardboard for master templates

For the patchwork: To do the whole range of objects, and even if you use a fairly large basket, 50 cm (½ yd) of the blue printed fabric and of the plain green should be sufficient. You will need about 90 cm (1 yd) of the light-coloured, printed fabric. If you use a fabric with a white ground which will be mounted on white fabric, as I have done, make sure that the two whites go well together.

N.B. All seam allowances, including patchwork, are 6 mm (¼ in).

1) Using the pattern shown below, make a master template out of cardboard and cut 76 paper templates. Refer to instructions for English Patchwork on page 128. The drawing below right shows the arrangement of the blue, green and light-coloured triangles. Note that the light-coloured triangles have been used together to form lozenges. They are also the ones that are appliquéd over the white background of the cushion, which is why it is essential that the shades of white are compatible.

Below left. *The coloured portion of the drawing gives you the exact size for the master to be used for cutting the paper templates. The outer line is the cutting line for the cloth.*

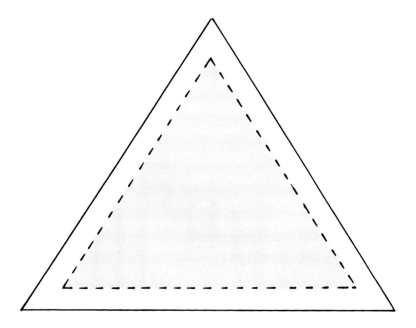

L: light, B: blue, G: green

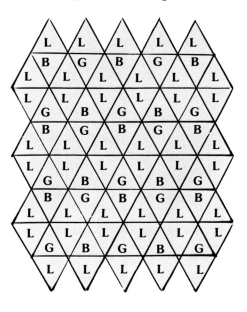

2) Cut and tack 46 light-coloured triangles, 16 out of the blue printed fabric and 14 out of the plain green. Make up the piece of patchwork. Press and remove tacking and paper templates. Make sure the turnovers on the outside pieces of the patchwork, which will be appliquéd over the cushion, are crisp and firmly pressed so that they do not lose their shape.

Above. *This drawing shows the arrangement of the triangles on the cushion.*

3) Lay the piece of prepared patchwork right side up over the square piece of white fabric. Centre it. Pin and tack in position, then carefully slip-stitch all around the patchwork, making sure that your stitches do not show on the right side.

4) Trim the excess cloth around the top of the cushion, leaving a 6 mm (¼ in) seam allowance beyond the points of the patchwork.

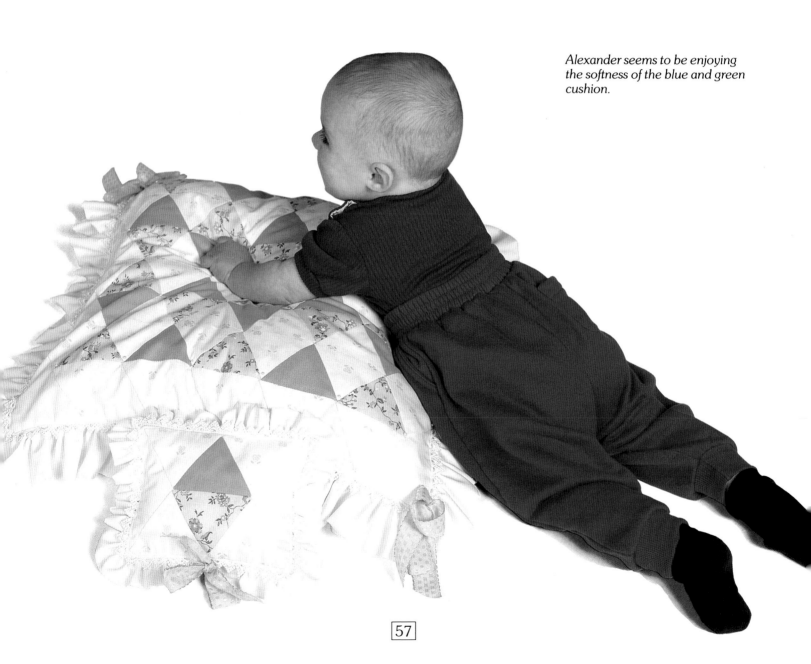

Alexander seems to be enjoying the softness of the blue and green cushion.

5) Prepare the frill by joining the cloth wherever necessary to make up a continuous strip. Machine-stitch the ends. Press the seams open. Fold the strip in half and press flat. Gather the frill by hand or on the sewing machine, 6 mm (¼ in) away from the raw edge of the fabric. Measure the perimeter of the cushion and tighten the gathers to the required length. Distribute the gathers evenly. Pin and tack the frill to the front of the cushion. Machine-stitch all round.

6) Take the oblong of white material. Trim excess cloth so that the *shorter* dimensions of the rectangles are the same length as the sides of the cushion. Fold the oblong into 2 (with the shorter sides together) and cut along the fold. As can be seen in the sketch opposite, the excess cloth will form an overlap at the centre of the back of the cushion, which can be left open to remove the pad or fastened with buttons, popper fasteners or a strip of Velcro tape.

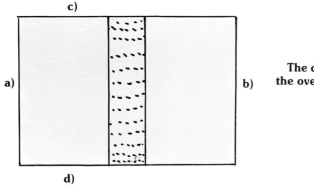

The dotted area represents the overlap at the centre of the pillowcase.

7) Lay the 2 pieces of white fabric over the front of the cushion, right sides together. Pin sides (a) together and machine-stitch, making sure that the frill does not get caught in the seam. Repeat for sides (b).

8) Make a narrow hem along the edges of the central overlap – the wrong side of the hem should face you. Pin sides (c) and (d) of cushion, making sure that the overlap lies flat. Machine-stitch.

9) Fix buttons, poppers or Velcro tape along the opening if desired. Turn the cushion cover inside out and press. Pin and slip-stitch the lace at the very edge of the cushion so that it lies over the frill. If you start in the corner, the joint will be hidden by one of the bows of ribbon. Attach the ribbons firmly and make 2 bows.

YOU WILL NEED

For the basket:

Enough of the white polycotton, lawn or other material used for the base of the cushion to line the inside of the basket and make the double-thickness skirt, which should be twice or even 2½ times the circumference of the basket. The depth of the skirt is determined by the height of the basket.

Enough of the narrow lace to go round the top of the basket and the bottom of the skirt

Enough of the ribbon specified for the cushion to go round the top of the basket and at least 1 extra metre (1¼ yd) to make 2 bows

1 piece of lightweight polyester wadding large enough to line the inside of the basket and overlap the edge

White thread

Toning thread for the patchwork

Stiff paper for templates and cardboard for master templates

For the patchwork: To look good, the skirt must be full. The bigger the basket, the fuller the skirt – you could still be making the patchwork by the time the child is 3 years old. Remember this when purchasing the basket!

N.B. All seam allowances, unless otherwise specified, are 6 mm (¼ in).

1) Line the inside of the basket with wadding. Press it to the bottom and smooth it around the sides and over the edge of the basket till you are satisfied with the way it sits. Run some stitches through the wickerwork to hold the wadding in place. Trim off excess wadding.

2) With newspaper make a paper template before cutting the white material which will line the inside of the basket. The basket I bought is hexagonal with a flat bottom and it widens towards the top – making a pattern of these rather complicated shapes was vital. Cut a piece of white material to fit the bottom over the wadding, leaving 20 mm (¾ in) seam allowance. Then cut a strip long enough and

wide enough to fit the circumference of the basket and its height. The lining should overlap the top of the basket and include a generous seam allowance. (Refer to the photograph of the basket on page 54.) Join this strip together along the shorter dimension. I had to gather mine slightly at the base to fit around the smaller hexagon which forms the bottom of the basket. Distribute the gathers evenly, if you have to do this. Pin and machine-stitch, right sides together, to the bottom piece. Fit inside the basket, allowing extra cloth to hang over the edge.

3) The skirt is made of a double thickness of material as shown in the sketch below. The patchwork border consists of 2 rows of triangles which, in the case of my basket, neatly fitted the height of the skirt. If you use a taller basket, you could add another row of triangles or set the border at the bottom of the skirt, leaving the top white.

4) Start by making the required length of patchwork. Make sure that you end with a green triangle if you started with a blue, so that when the skirt is joined up at the side, the patchwork pattern is uninterrupted and hides the seam neatly. This is why it is advisable to make the patchwork first, then cut the length of the skirt to fit the pattern, rather than cutting through the patchwork to fit the skirt. Make the side seam on the skirt before starting to appliqué the patchwork. Press the seam open – the wrong side of the patchwork should of course be laid over the right side of the skirt.

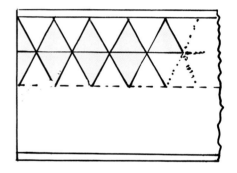

This diagram shows the arrangement of the diamonds on the basket border.

5) Appliqué the patchwork to the skirt as explained for the Cushion. Press. Then fold the skirt in half as shown on the diagram. Press the bottom edge flat.

6) Pin or tack the 2 edges of the 'waist' of the skirt together. Run a line of gathers by hand or machine 6 mm (¼ in) from raw edge. Tighten to the length required to fit the top of the basket lining. Distribute gathers evenly. You will now use some of the ribbon to bind the top of the skirt. Pin the ribbon over the gathers, right sides together. Machine-stitch close to the edge of the ribbon. Turn ribbon over and hem-stitch, making sure you cover the gathers.

7) Slip-stitch the skirt to the overhanging edge of the basket lining. With an awkwardly shaped basket such as the one I had chosen, it is easier to do this with the lining in place inside the basket. Do not forget to leave gaps to fit over the handles, if applicable. I fitted mine over the handles, then slip-stitched the gaps loosely. This means that these few stitches will need to be snipped off when I want to remove the basket cover for washing, and replaced afterwards. If you decide to

go that route, finish off the basket completely before closing the gaps between the handles. The alternative is to bind the edge of the basket lining along the openings with a little more of the blue ribbon. This takes longer to do and does not look as pretty for a small object. This is the method I used around the handles of the Moses Basket (*see* page 88). Obviously, the cover of the Moses Basket will need frequent washing. Once the skirt is attached to the lining, trim off excess cloth and neaten the seam.

8) Slip-stitch the lace over the top edge of the patchwork border. Hand- or machine-stitch more lace at the very edge of the skirt.

9) Place the cover over the basket. Slip-stitch the gap loosely over the handles. Attach lengths of ribbon near the handles and make bows.

YOU WILL NEED

For the pincushion

White fabric: 4 offcuts 190 × 150 mm (7½ × 6 in) each of polycotton, lawn or other material

1 strip 1.60 m × 75 mm (1¾ yd × 3 in) for the frill. This too can be joined

Polyester filling for the inside of the cushion

Narrow lace: 90 cm (1 yd)

Ribbon: 50 cm (20 in) as specified for Cushion

White thread

Toning thread for patchwork

Stiff paper for templates and cardboard for master templates.

N.B. All seam allowances, including patchwork, are 6 mm (¼ in).

Patchwork piece ready for mounting on to the top of the pincushion.

1) Make a piece of patchwork as shown opposite. Appliqué it to one of the oblongs of white material as explained for the large cushion. Trim excess cloth, leaving a 6 mm (¼ in) seam allowance beyond the points of the patchwork. Take the second oblong of white fabric and trim it to exactly the

same size as the front of the pincushion. This will form the back of the pincushion. Keep to one side.

2) Make up the frill in the same way as for the large cushion and attach it to the front of the pincushion. With right sides together, pin the back of the pincushion to the front. Machine-stitch, leaving one short side open. Make sure the frill is not caught up in the seam. Slip-stitch the lace at the edge of the cushion so that it lies over the frill.

3) Take the remaining 2 oblongs of white fabric. They will form the pad inside the pincushion. The pad should be about 15 mm (½ in) bigger in both directions than the inside of the pincushion. Add a 6 mm (¼ in) seam allowance and trim off excess cloth. Machine-stitch, leaving one short dimension open. Insert the polyester filling, making sure that it is well pushed into the corners of the pad. Slip-stitch the open end by hand. Slip into the pincushion cover. Slip-stitch the open side of the cover (you can wash the pincushion with the pad inside it). Attach a length of ribbon to hide the join in the lace, make a bow.

YOU WILL NEED

For the cotton wool bag

White fabric: 1 piece 280 × 495 mm (11 × 19¼ in)

White polyester dress lining: 1 piece 280 × 495 mm (11 × 19¼ in)

Narrow lace: 1 m (1¼ yd)

Ribbon: 90 cm (1 yd), as specified for Cushion

White thread

Toning thread for patchwork

Stiff paper for templates and cardboard for master templates

N.B. All seam allowances, including patchwork, are 6 mm (¼ in).

1) The border is made in exactly the same way as that of the Basket. It has 6 light-coloured triangles at the top. Make up the length of patchwork. Lay it over the oblong of white material, leaving a 6 mm (¼ in) seam allowance at the bottom below the points of the patchwork. Leave the same allowance for the side of the bag and trim off excess cloth.

2) Lay this flat piece of fabric over the oblong of lining. Trim lining to exactly the same size and keep to one side.

3) Pin and machine-stitch the side seam of the bag. Press seam open and position it at the centre of the back of the bag. Appliqué the patchwork in the usual manner, making sure that 3 complete diamonds appear at the front of the bag. (See photograph on page 54.) Press.

4) Slip-stitch or machine-stitch the lace over the top edge of the patchwork. Machine-stitch the bottom of the bag.

5) Machine-stitch the side seam of the lining. Press the seam open and position it in the middle of the back. Machine-stitch the bottom seam. Press. With the right sides together, pin the top of the lining to the top of the bag, leaving a 75 mm (3 in) gap for turning the work inside out. Turn over and press the top of the bag flat. Slip-stitch the opening.

6) Run a line of machine stitches 50 mm (2 in) from the top of the bag and another row 20 mm (¾ in) below the first. This will form a channel for the ribbon to go through. At the front of the bag, cut a vertical slit through the top fabric of the channel (do not pierce the lining). The ribbon will be threaded through this opening. Neaten the edges with button-hole stitches.

7) Machine-stitch or slip-stitch by hand a row of lace at the very edge of the top of the bag. Thread the ribbon through the channel and make a bow.

Pram Quilt & Pillowcase

This quilt and its matching pillowcase have been made entirely with silks as the set was conceived as an elegant christening present. It uses two different cream-coloured silks of different textures (see detail on page 67). The quilt would look equally attractive made of lawns or other cotton fabrics and would be more practical for everyday use. A subtle contrast could be achieved by using a smooth cream-coloured cotton and a textured one. The technique used is American Seamed Patchwork (see page 129 for instructions). It is made entirely on the machine.

YOU WILL NEED

For the quilt:

Cream base fabric: 1.30 m (1½ yd) of smooth silk or smooth-textured lawn or cotton, 90 cm (36 in) wide

Cream fabric for details: 30 cm (12 in) of raw silk or textured cotton material, 90 cm (36 in) wide

Lightweight polyester wadding: 60 cm (¾ yd) in 96 cm (38 in) width

Toning polyester thread

Toning silk or other thread for hand quilting (depending on type of fabrics used)

Cardboard for templates

Pencil-shaped tailor's chalk (optional)

For the patchwork stars: You will need scraps of silks or other fabrics in 'families': ranging from mauve to purple; pale yellow to orange; shell pink to shocking pink; pale blues to dark blues; pale greens to dark greens. The diamond shapes

The size of the finished quilt is 55 × 49 cm
(21$\frac{1}{2}$ × 19$\frac{1}{2}$ in) and that of the pillowcase
is 37 × 48 cm (14$\frac{1}{2}$ × 19 in).

on the quilt are made of the cream raw silk. The main part of the quilt and its backing are made of smooth cream silk. The contrast is obtained by using the cream raw silk as part of the design and on the corner squares with the quilted stars. Refer to the diagram opposite for guidance. Textured cotton can be substituted for raw silk.

N.B. All seam allowances, including patchwork, are 6 mm (¼ in).

1) From the shapes on the right, cut 3 master templates. You will need 72 diamond shapes – 6 for each star; cut colours accordingly. Out of the cream raw silk or textured cotton cut 48 of the large triangles, and 144 small triangles out of the smooth cream-coloured silk or lawn. If you are using silk, you will find that it frays very easily. In order to avoid this make sure that you handle the cut pieces as little as possible. After cutting the pieces, store them in a stiff envelope with 2 sides cut open, or attach them to a polystyrene sheet with fine lace pins. It is a bit like making pastry – the less you handle, the better the end product! Use a dry iron when you press the silks or the finished patchwork. Silk can stand very high temperatures, but may mark if droplets of water fall on it.

2) Following the instructions for American Seamed Patchwork on page 129, make up 12 blocks. Follow the diagram on page 69 for the order of assembly. Press each seam as you go along.

3) Measure the patchwork along its long and short dimensions. This will give you the length of the border pieces – the width is that of the square corner pieces – as shown on the template on page 67 (right). Cut the 4 border pieces out of the smooth cream silk or lawn.

4) Make a cardboard template based on the pattern opposite and cut the 4 corner pieces out of the cream raw silk or textured cotton.

5) Pin the long border pieces, right sides together, to the long dimensions of the patchwork. Machine-stitch. Pin and machine-stitch the corner squares at either end of the shorter border pieces. Pin and machine-stitch these 2 strips along the shorter sides of the patchwork. Press, folding the seams under the patchwork.

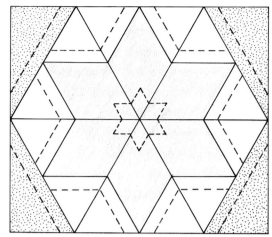

Arrangement of raw, smooth & coloured silks

smooth cream silk

cream raw silk

coloured silk

quilting line

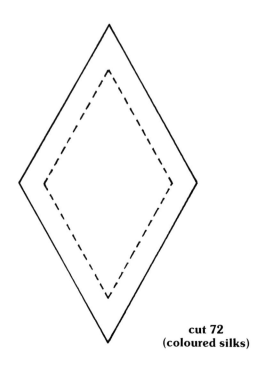

**cut 72
(coloured silks)**

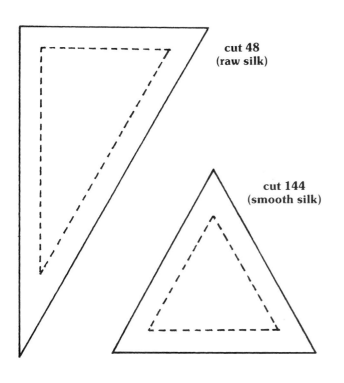

cut 48
(raw silk)

cut 144
(smooth silk)

6) Lay the piece of smooth cream silk or lawn, which will form the back of the quilt, face down on the table. Put the wadding on top and lay the prepared front of the quilt, face up, over it. Pin to hold the layers together and trim backing and wadding to the same size as the quilt top. Tack all 3 layers together as described in the instructions for basic quilting on page 136, No. 2.

7) Begin the hand-quilting, working from the centre of the quilt. The broken line on the diagram at the top of page 66 shows where the quilting lines run. The lines are positioned 6 mm (¼ in) away from the seams and basically follow the star design. If you don't feel confident to work them freehand, draw these lines as you go along, using a well-sharpened tailor's chalk and holding the quilt taut under your fingers. Do not forget to quilt the star shapes inside the patchwork stars and on the 4 corner pieces.

8) Binding the edge of the quilt. Heirloom quilts were traditionally finished off with a double binding. The golden rule is to use a strip of fabric 6 times the finished width, cut on the straight grain of the fabric. As it is quite difficult to cut slippery silk accurately, make yourself a cardboard

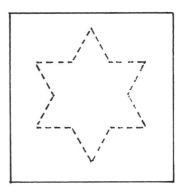

Pattern for the corner squares template. The dotted line is the quilting line around the star motif.

template using the shape shown opposite. Use it to mark the silk along the grain with a sharp tailor's chalk, prior to cutting. (Refer to the binding section on page 137 to see how to attach the binding and mitre the corners.)

YOU WILL NEED

Cream base fabric: 1.10 m (1¼ yd) of smooth silk or smooth textured lawn or cotton, 90 cm (36 in) wide

Cream fabric for details: Offcut of raw silk or textured cotton material left over from the Quilt

Left-over threads from the Quilt

3 plastic popper fasteners or narrow ribbon for ties (optional)

Cardboard for templates

Pencil-shaped tailor's chalk (optional)

For the patchwork: Scraps of coloured silks left over from the matching Quilt.

N.B. All seam allowances, including patchwork, are 6 mm (¼ in).

1) Using the templates you made for the Quilt and following the diagram shown at the top of page 70, prepare a strip of patchwork comprising 3 half-star motifs in the yellow, green and pink ranges. Press.

2) Measure the lengths of the finished patchwork border. Use this measurement to cut an oblong of smooth cream-coloured silk or lawn to a depth of 240 mm (9½ in). (For cutting, position the long dimension of the oblong along the selvedge of the fabric.) Pin and machine-stitch this panel along the length of the patchwork strip to form the front of the pillowcase. Press and fold the seam under the patchwork.

This template shows the width of the strip required to bind the quilt. The length you need is 2.20 m (2½ yd).

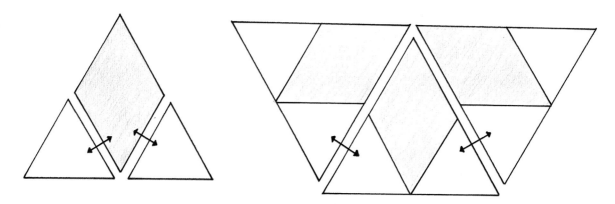

white areas: smooth silk
dotted areas: raw silk
pink areas: coloured silk

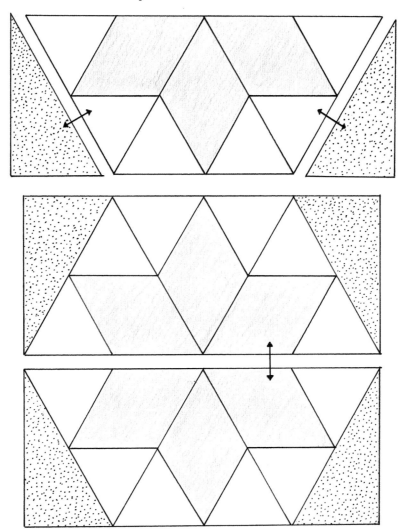

This diagram shows the order in which the pieces of fabric are assembled to form a block. The principle is to join straight lines with straight lines.

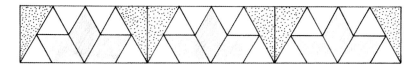

patchwork border for the pillowcase

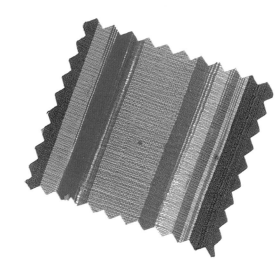

3) The front of the pillowcase needs to be lined to cover the wrong side of the patchwork. You also need to cut a piece for the back of the pillowcase, measuring 38 × 80 cm (15 × 31½ in). Use the front of the pillowcase to give you the meaurements for its lining. N.B. Cut both pieces out of paper first and position them on the remaining piece of smooth cream-coloured silk or lawn to make sure you cut in an economical manner and leave yourself enough cloth for the border strips. Keep the larger oblong (for the back of the pillowcase) to one side.

4) With wrong sides together, pin and tack the front of the pillowcase to its lining. Also run a line of tacking immediately below the edge of the patchwork border. Quilt the motifs, referring to No. 7 of the instructions for the silk Quilt on page 67.

5) Using the square template you made for the Quilt, cut the 4 corner pieces out of the cream raw silk or textured cotton. Measure the dimensions of the front of the pillowcase. These will determine the lengths of the border strips, which should be the same width as the corner squares. Cut the border strips.

6) Pin and machine-stitch the 2 longer strips to the front of the pillowcase, right sides together. Pin and machine-stitch the corner squares to either end of the shorter border strips. Pin and machine-stitch to the pillow case. Press.

7) To fix the back of the pillowcase and finish off the overlap, follow instructions for the blue and green Cushion from No. 6 to 8 on page 58.

8) To finish off, top-stitch the front of the pillowcase to the back as close as possible to the edge of the border strip.

9) Quilt the star motif on the corner squares.

*This colourful Seminole Jacket made a perfect autumn outfit for
Alexander Osborne. See instructions on page 80.*

Changing Bag
with Detachable Mat

T his is a vital piece of equipment which enables you to pack and carry all of baby's requirements and also to change him or her, wherever you may be. The bag and its mat are made in the popular American log-cabin design which is sewn on the machine. It uses the attractive 'straight furrow' arrangement which contrasts parallel bands of light and dark patchwork. I deliberately chose 'adult' colours when selecting fabrics for this item, after listening to the common complaint that most commercial versions of this bag tend to come in pastel colours and animal prints. These may look pretty in baby's room but they do not complement mum's clothes. The bag and the mat are entirely lined with waterproof material. The mat fits over the bag (see page 77) and is attached to it with heavy-duty-press-fasteners. Inside the bag are roomy pockets, also made of the waterproof material.

The changing mat can be produced as a gift in its own right, in which case, omit the fasteners. The tumbling-block bib, seen here draped over the bag, uses some of the prints used for the bag and tones up nicely with it. (To make this bib, refer to instructions on page 50.)

YOU WILL NEED

Bag: 1 m (1 yd) of 90 cm (36 in) wide fine white cotton to back the patchwork squares

Mat: 70 cm (¾ yd) of the same

Bag: 1.10 m (1¼ yd) of 115 cm (45 in) wide waterproof lining (e.g. shower curtaining)

Mat: 60 cm (¾ yd) of the same

Base and sides of bag: 30 cm (12 in) of 90 cm (36 in) wide heavy-duty furnishing sew-in interfacing

Bag: 2 m (2½ yd) of toning canvas webbing
  1 zip, 55 cm (22 in) long

Mat: 60 cm (¾ yd) of lightweight polyester wadding
  3 m (3¼ yd) of wide cotton bias binding

Bag/Mat: 8 heavy-duty hammer-on press fasteners

Toning thread Piece of cardboard for template

Washable fabric marker

*Changing bag with detachable mat, all
lined with waterproof material. Finished
size of the bag: 35 × 53 cm (14 × 21 in).*

Prepare 12 squares for the bag
and 15 for the mat.

For the patchwork: You will need scraps of printed cotton or 30 cm (⅓ yd) each of some 18 different patterns, half in dark and half in light tones. For the centre squares, if you make them all in *one* shade of yellow, you will need 30 cm (⅓ yd). Alternatively, use a variety of yellow scraps as I have done. The technique used for the bag and the mat is machine-sewn Log Cabin Patchwork. Basic instructions for this appear on page 130.

N.B. All seam allowances, including patchwork: 6 mm (¼ in).

1) The bag. Make a cardboard template by copying the pattern opposite left. Cut 12 squares out of the white cotton material and transfer the sewing lines marked on the template, using a washable fabric marker. (Refer to the basic instructions for Log Cabin Patchwork on page 130.) I have used the popular 'straight-furrow' pattern.

2) Make a cardboard template by copying the pattern opposite right and cut 12 yellow/orange squares.

3) Make a cardboard template by copying the pattern on page 76 and cut light and dark strips of fabric. Machine-stitch as instructed on page 130. Make up 12 blocks.

4) Arrange the blocks to your satisfaction, assemble to form 2 panels of 2 × 3 blocks each (front and back of the bag).

5) Base of bag and gussets. Make a cardboard template by copying the pattern on page 78 and cut 30 of these larger strips in an assortment of colours. Add up the dimensions of 1 long side and 2 short sides of one of the patchwork panels. This will give you the length of the band of fabric required to make the base of the bag and its gussets. Cut a strip of fine white cotton to that length – its width should be the length of one of the rectangular strips you have just cut. This will form the base of the patchwork.

6) Arrange the 30 strips on a table in the order you want to use them. Lay the first coloured strip, right side up, at the top end of the backing strip. Stitch where shown on the diagram. Take the next colour strip and lay it face down over the first. Stitch where shown on the diagram. Fold the second piece down flat. Press and repeat the process, until you have covered the strip of white fabric.

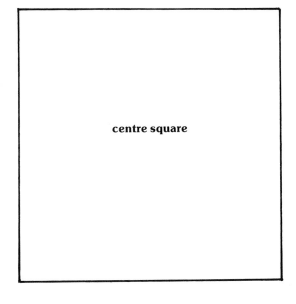

centre square

Page 74. Use this pattern to cut the 12 squares of white cotton backing. Transfer the sewing lines with a fabric marker.

Above. *Use this template for cutting the 12 yellow/orange squares.*

7) Trim both sides of the patchwork strip to ensure that the edges are straight and to reduce the width of the strip to 14 cm (5½ in). Run a line of stitches all around the strip to prevent the patchwork from coming undone.

8) Measure the length of the top of the bag and cut a strip of the white fabric to the same width as before. Cut a further 13 pieces in an assortment of colours, and proceed as in No. 5 and 6 above. Make up the piece of patchwork to fit the top of the bag and trim it down to 14 cm (5½ in) wide as before. Cut the strip in 2 halves lengthwise. Run a line of stitching all around each strip to prevent the patchwork from coming undone. Insert the zip between the 2 strips (see basic instructions on page 140).

9) With right sides together, pin, tack and machine-stitch the 2 Log Cabin panels to the zipped top of the bag. Press.

10) With right sides together, pin or tack the long strip which will form the sides and base of the bag around the 3 open sides of the front panel. Machine-stitch. Please note that in order to go round the corners of the gusset neatly, you need to ease the fabric by clipping the corners close to the seam of the gusset strip.

11) Open the zip, turn the bag inside out and assemble the back panel as before.

12) Out of the interfacing, cut 3 strips to fit the sides and base of the bag *flush up to the seams*. Slip-stitch them into position.

13) The carrying strap made of webbing is attached to the gussets of the bag by top-stitching. Make a 25 mm (1 in) turnover at one end and pin it approximately 150 mm (6 in) from the base of the bag, centred on the gusset. Work 2 rows of top-stitching 6 mm (¼ in) apart around the strap, up to the point where it reaches the top of the bag. Sling the bag over your shoulder to check the length required for the strap. Trim off any excess and pin and machine-stitch that end as before.

14) Lining. Out of the waterproof fabric, cut 2 oblongs 375 × 555 mm (14¾ × 21¾ in). Cut 2 strips for the sides of the bag measuring 134 × 555 mm (5¼ × 21¾ in). Make

yourself paper patterns, *including* the pockets described below, and arrange them on the fabric to find the most economical way to cut it. The 2 pockets each measure 280 × 555 mm (11 × 21¾ in).

15) Make a narrow hem at the edge of both pockets. Pin one pocket, right side of hem on top, over the bottom part of the front panel of the lining. Repeat the process for the back panel. Work out how many compartments you want to have in the pockets and run vertical lines of stitching, as shown in the diagram at the bottom of page 78. You can now attach the panels to the sides and base of the lining as you did for the bag.

A corner of the mat has been turned over to reveal the waterproof material and the hammer-on poppers which attach the mat to the bag.

**Use this template to cut
the strips to form the gussets
of the bag.**

16) Fitting the lining. Open the bag and insert the lining into position, wrong sides together. Turn over the edges at the top of the lining – 6 mm (¼ in) – and pin to the edges of the zip. Slip-stitch into place.

N.B. It is advisable to complete the mat before attempting to fit the hammer-on poppers to the bag.

THE MAT

1) Make up 15 blocks of Log Cabin Patchwork as explained for the bag. Assemble them as before. Be particularly careful with your colour arrangement, as the straight-furrow pattern will stand out much more clearly on a large flat piece such as the mat.

2) Lay the finished patchwork face up over the wadding. Trim wadding to size. Pin and tack the 2 layers together. Attach the patchwork to the wadding by working a few hand stitches at the corners of each block, using toning thread. If you sew 'in the ditch' – in the crease of the seam – the stitches won't show.

3) Lay the patchwork face up over the waterproof material and trim the latter to size. Tack the 3 layers together all round. Bind the edges with wide bias binding, mitring the corners as you go (see instructions on page 137).

4) If you have made the mat to go with the bag, this is the time to fit the poppers. Drape the mat over the bag. Carefully mark with pins the position of the poppers at the front, the back and under the base of the bag. Mark the corresponding places on the mat and fix the poppers according to the manufacturer's instructions.

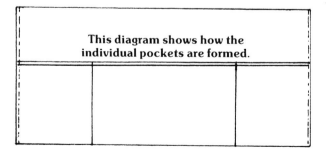

**This diagram shows how the
individual pockets are formed.**

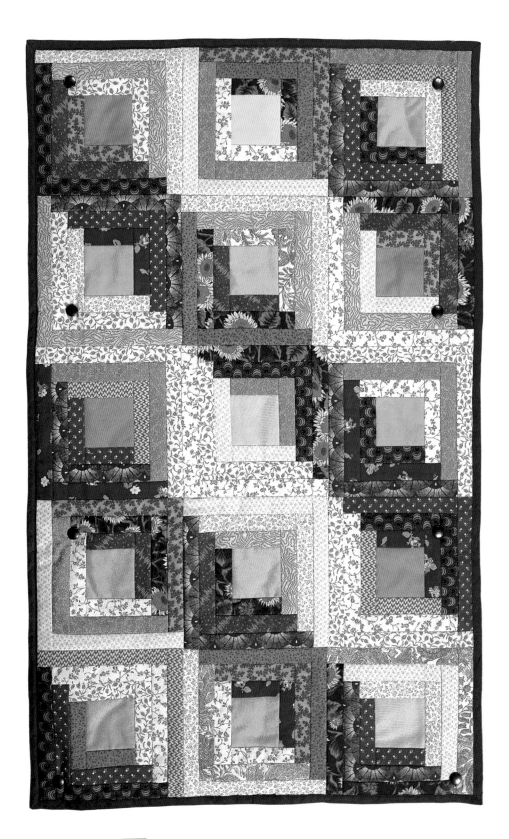

When the mat is shown flat, the 'straight-furrow' pattern becomes even more apparent. Size of finished mat: 92 × 55 cm (36 × 22 in).

Unisex Seminole Jackets

The Seminoles were a group of native Americans who lived in the Everglades of southern Florida. At the beginning of the 20th century, traders introduced the sewing machine to them. The women soon developed a wonderful way of creating richly coloured cloth by sewing contrasting strips together, cutting across to form diamond and triangle shapes and joining those strips again to produce a continuous piece of fabric. I think the technique is particularly apt for these chunky quilted jackets, which look equally good on girls and on boys. I worked the jacket in two colourways, using heavier fabrics for the larger one.

YOU WILL NEED

For the patchwork: 50 cm (½ yd) each of 4 contrasting/ co-ordinating fabrics, 90 cm (36 in) wide

Suggested fabrics: cotton or polyester cotton for a lighter weight jacket and brushed cotton, light wool and needlecord for a more wintery garment

Lining:

Size:	6 months	12 months	18 months
Fabric width: 115 cm 45 in	60 cm ¾ yd	65 cm ¾ yd	65 cm ¾ yd
150 cm 60 in	40 cm ½ yd	45 cm ½ yd	45 cm ½ yd

Butter muslin: 1 m (1 yd)

Lightweight polyester wadding: 70 cm (¾ yd)

Fold-over binding: 2.50m (¾ yd)

4 13 mm (½ in) diameter buttons

Toning thread

The smaller jacket at the bottom was worked in crisp cottons. It has fabric-covered buttons and you can see it being worn by Alexander, then aged 6 months, on page 33.

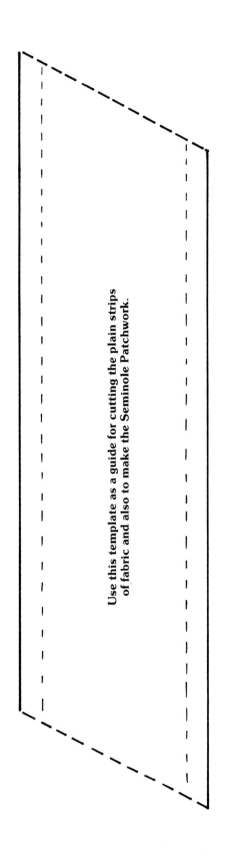

Use this template as a guide for cutting the plain strips of fabric and also to make the Seminole Patchwork.

N.B. The patchwork seam allowance is 6 mm (¼ in), as marked on the templates. The seam allowance for the garment itself is 15 mm (⅝ in) – see pattern on page 86.

1) Using the pattern on the left and the 2 triangular ones on the page opposite, make 3 master templates. Use the long one to enable you to cut strips out of 3 of your chosen fabrics. Refer to the instructions for Seminole Patchwork on page 132. You will need a total length of 234 cm (92 in), but this can be made up in more than one section.

2) Join the 3 strips, then using the same template as before, mark across the strips and cut into sections (see No. 2, page 132). You will need 14 sections for the back of the jacket, 16 for the front and 12 for the sleeves.

3) Now reposition the cut sections as in No. 3 a) on page 132. Pin, carefully matching seams, then machine-stitch 6 mm (¼ in) away from the raw edges as before – see No. 3 b). Join 2 lots of 7 sections for the back of the jacket, 2 lots of 8 for the fronts and 2 lots of 6 for the sleeves. Lay the strips flat and, using a ruler and a washable fabric marker, draw a line 6 mm (¼ in) away from the centre of the first and the third row of diamonds as shown in No. 4 on page 132. (This will give you a seam allowance.) You should now have 1 row of diamonds with triangles on either side.

4) Using the same template as before, cut long strips from each of your 4 fabrics.

5) Join 3 strips to either side of the front patchwork panels and 4 to either side of those prepared for the sleeves. The length of these strips should be the same as that of their respective patchwork panels. Press the seams outwards from the patchwork. Refer to the photograph of the jacket if you are not sure how it should look.

6) For the back of the jacket make up the pin-wheel patchwork block, using the 2 triangular templates and following the instructions for American Seamed Patchwork on page 129. The diagram of the pin-wheel opposite is not shown real size – it is only there to help you to construct the pin-wheel pattern.

7) Join 3 short strips – top and bottom of the pin-wheel block. Join the Seminole strips on either side of this panel. Finally attach 3 vertical strips along the 2 Seminole bands. (One glance at the back of the jacket will make all this clear.) The finished patchwork for the back of the jacket should measure at least 34 × 36 cm (13½ × 14½ in).

8) For each sleeve join strips on either side of the Seminole strip. The finished pieces of patchwork should measure at least 40 × 33 cm (16 × 13 in).

9) For each piece of patchwork, i.e. 2 fronts, 1 back and 2 sleeves, cut the same size piece of wadding and muslin.

10) Lay the piece of muslin on a table top, put the corresponding wadding on top of it, then the patchwork, facing up. Pin and tack the layers together firmly, then quilt 'in the ditch' along the length of each seam where you joined the individual strips. Refer to No. 3 on page 136. Repeat for all the pieces.

11) On pages 86 to 87 you will find the pattern from which both jackets were made. As usual, you will need to enlarge it to 200% or trace it on to squared-up dress-maker's paper.

12) Place each piece of the pattern over its respective piece of patchwork. You will need to do this very carefully to ensure that the vertical lines *are* vertical and the 2 fronts and the 2 sleeves match each other.

13) You may have enough offcuts to make the pockets. If not, mount 3 strips of fabric and quilt as described. Cut out pockets according to the pattern and press under 15 mm (⅝ in) on side edges. Tack.

14) Apply fold-over binding to upper edges of both pockets.

15) Stay-stitch front neck edge 10 mm (⅜ in) from raw edge.

16) Pin pockets to the fronts of the jacket, matching upper corners to the dots. Machine-stitch close to the side edges of the pockets. Tack 6 mm (¼ in) from the lower edge.

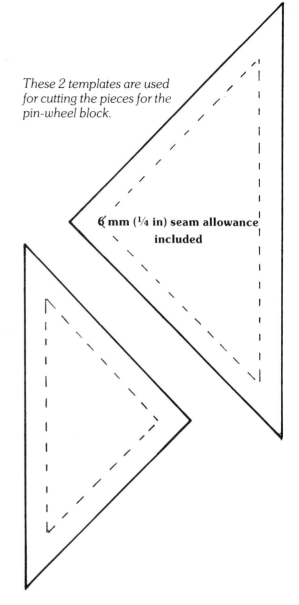

These 2 templates are used for cutting the pieces for the pin-wheel block.

6 mm (¼ in) seam allowance included

This diagram shows how the pin-wheel block is constructed.

17) Stay-stitch back neck edge. Machine-stitch jacket shoulder seam. Trim wadding as close to the seam as possible. Press seam lightly.

18) With right sides together, pin sleeve to armhole edge, placing centre dot to shoulder seam and matching remaining dots. Machine-stitch. Run another line of stitching 3 mm ($\frac{1}{8}$ in) away from the first and within the seam allowance. Trim seam below notches. Trim the wadding close to the seam. Press seam lightly towards the sleeve.

19) With right sides together, machine-stitch the entire underarm seam in one continuous seam. Trim wadding close to the seam. Press lightly.

20) Cut out and assemble the lining as described for the jacket.

21) With wrong sides together, place the lining inside the jacket and tack around all the edges.

22) Finish off the fronts and the bottom edge of the jacket with fold-over binding, starting and finishing at the neck edge. Repeat the operation around the neck and the edges of the sleeves. Turn the ends in neatly.

23) On the appropriate side, right for a girl and left for a boy, mark the position of the buttonholes and work them by hand or by machine.

24) Sew on the buttons on the opposite front of the jacket. For the smaller jacket I covered the buttons in cloth, using all 4 colours. Alternatively, buy buttons which match one of the fabrics used.

The pin-wheel pattern at the back of the jacket adds interest to the garment.

The pattern overleaf is reproduced half size. Each square represents 50 mm (2 in). Enlarge the design on a photocopier – 200% – or trace it carefully on to dress-making paper.

This is the larger jacket, front and back. We unrolled the sleeves to show how they are made up of individual stripes. For this version I used a mixture of brushed cotton, fine wool and needlecord. These chunkier fabrics have given an interesting texture to the garment. The darker colours also make it suitable for winter. Alexander, by then aged 15 months, models this second jacket on page 71.

The decorative potentials of Seminole Patchwork are endless. Using a check pattern in the centre stripe has added a further dimension to the centre diamonds.

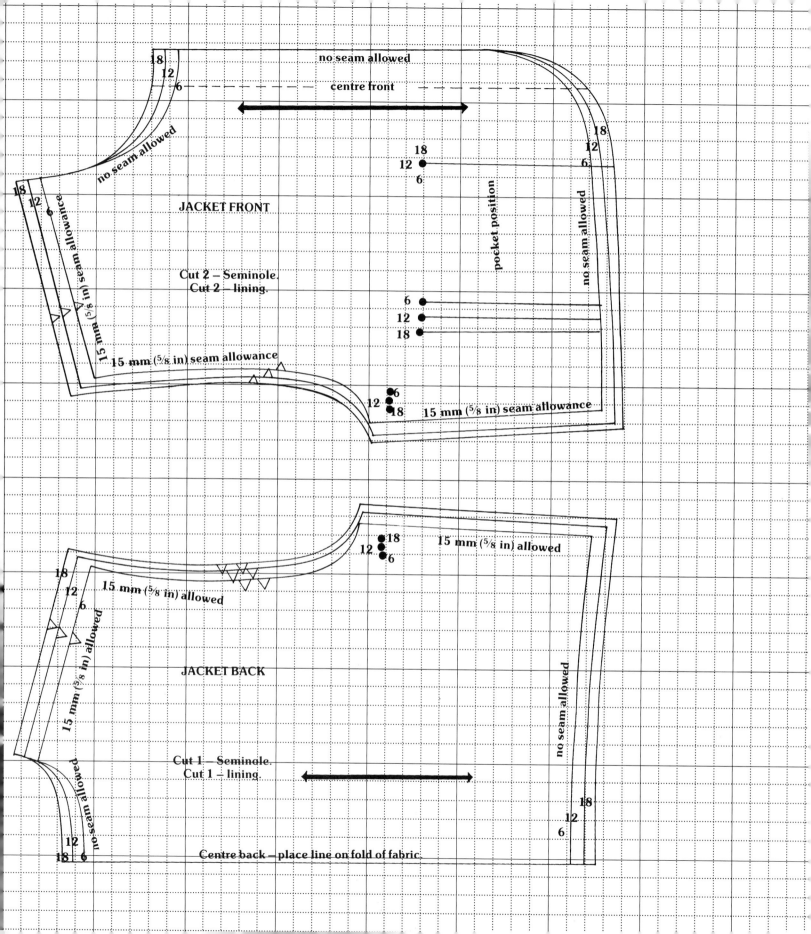

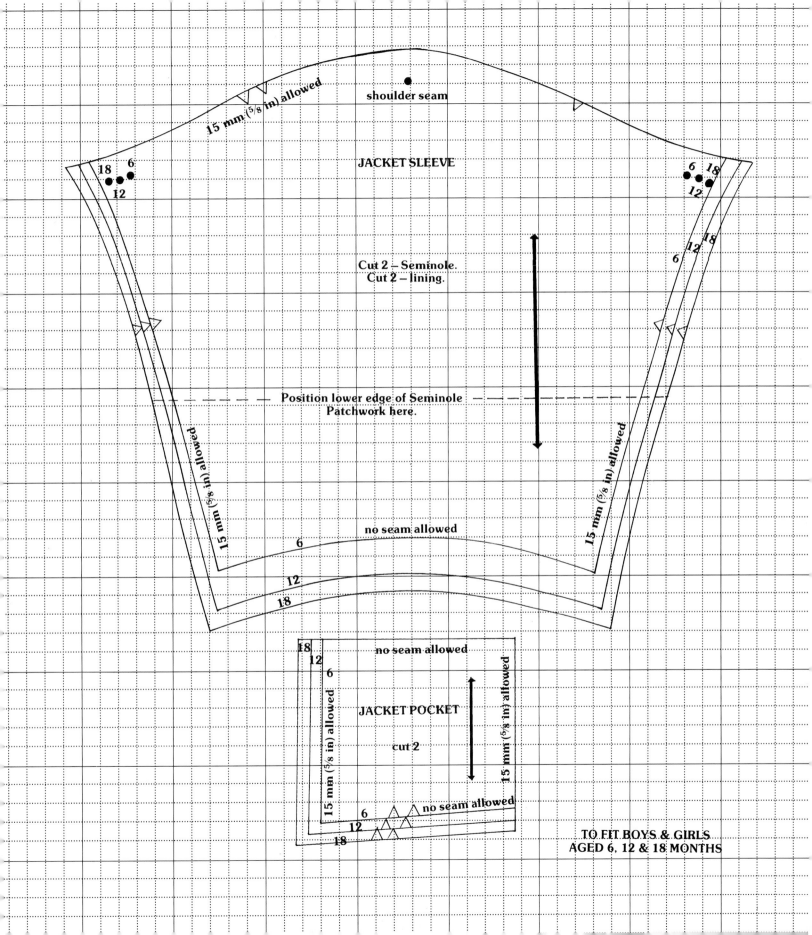

JACKET SLEEVE

15 mm (5⁄8 in) allowed

shoulder seam

18 6
12

6 18
12

18
12 6

Cut 2 – Seminole.
Cut 2 – lining.

Position lower edge of Seminole — — — — — — — —
Patchwork here.

15 mm (5⁄8 in) allowed

15 mm (5⁄8 in) allowed

no seam allowed

6

12

18

18
12

6

JACKET POCKET

cut 2

no seam allowed

15 mm (5⁄8 in) allowed

15 mm (5⁄8 in) allowed

6
12
18

no seam allowed

TO FIT BOYS & GIRLS
AGED 6, 12 & 18 MONTHS

Moses Basket

T he story of baby Moses being hidden among the reeds in the waters of Egypt inspired the decorative theme for this basket. I bought a very simple basket, covered it in Nile-green fabric and decorated it with appliquéd lotus flowers and the spade-like leaves of bulrushes. The geometric border is made of American Seamed Patchwork. See page 129 for general instructions on this technique.

YOU WILL NEED

Main colour fabric: 2 m (2 yd) of plain polycotton sheeting, 228 cm (90 in) wide

Medium-weight polyester wadding: 1.50 m (60 in) in 90 cm (36 in) width

Matching and toning threads

Ribbon: 90 cm (1 yd) in 20 mm (¾ in) width

Bias tape: 90 cm (1 yd)

Narrow cotton tape: 90 cm (1 yd)

Paper-backed fusible web

Stiff paper

A plain Moses basket

A Moses basket is the best present with which to welcome a new baby into the world. Make sure to have it ready by the time the child is born as the basket is outgrown all too soon.

Four-week-old Juliet cosily ensconced in her Moses basket. The fresh colours of the coverings complimented her dark hair and eyes.

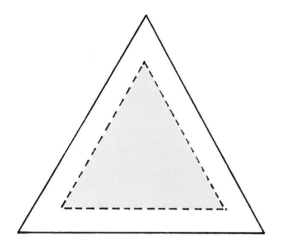

For the appliquéd leaves of the bulrushes you will need 25 cm (10 in) each of 3 or 4 different green cotton fabrics, and for the lotus flowers 25 cm (10 in) each of pink and turquoise cotton cloth. **For the patchwork border**, the stalks and petals of the flowers you will need an assortment of toning scraps of printed and plain cotton fabrics.

Above. *This is the template used in the patchwork border. The pattern pieces on the page opposite are shown half size. You can enlarge them on a photocopier (200%) or trace them on to squared-up paper. Each large square is the equivalent of 5 cm (2 in).*

Below. *This detail of the basket shows the arrangement of the 'reeds' which will frame the baby's head.*

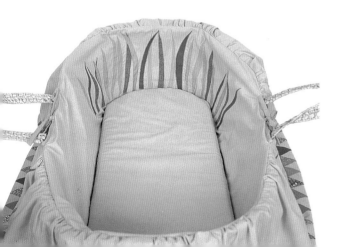

1) Moses baskets are not standard in size and you will need to make a paper pattern for the inside of the basket and a cover for the little mattress which normally fits inside it. Allow 1.5 cm (5/8 in) seam allowance all round. Line the basket with wadding (refer to instructions 1) and 2) on pages 59-60).

2) Cut a piece of polycotton to line the sides of the basket. You will probably need to cut this in 2 halves, so remember to add 1.5 cm (5/8 in) seam allowance wherever necessary. Join the two halves together at the head of the basket.

3) To make the skirt of the basket, take the pattern you made for the inside and double its length. Add an extra 2.5 cm (1 in) to the lower edge. Cut the skirt in 2 halves out of the polycotton material, adding 1.5 cm (5/8 in) for each seam. Join the 2 halves with a seam. Press open.

4) Enlarge the complete pattern shown on page 91. Using stiff paper, cut out the leaf shapes and cut 24 'reeds' out of your various green fabrics. Turn to the instructions for appliqué on page 135.

5) Position the leaves on the right side of the fabric, along the head end of the inside lining of the basket. Make sure they are high enough so that the mattress and the baby's head will not hide them. Iron into position and satin-stitch around the leaves (see page 135).

6) Machine-stitch the foot end of the inside lining strip. Press seam open. You can now join this inside lining strip to the piece which will cover the base of the basket. Pin with right sides together, easing any fullness in the inside strip with little tucks. Tack and machine-stitch.

90

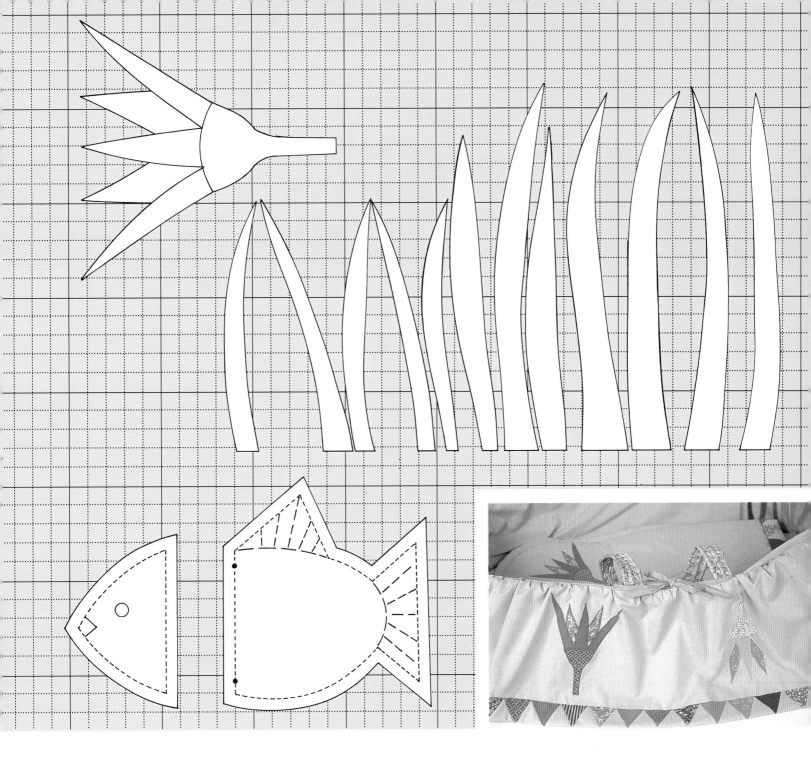

The fish

------- sewing line   — — — — quilting line

-•----•- Pin 'fin' between dots.

Use patchwork template to cut fin.

The photographic detail shows the bias-bound gaps around the handles of the basket and the way ribbons have been attached on either side and tied into bows.

7) Using your enlarged version of the pattern provided, cut a paper template of the lotus flower. Prepare 11 flowers, using the plain and printed fabrics to best effect. Back, fix and embroider them as you did for the reeds.

8) The length of the patchwork border which edges the skirt is dependent on the fullness of the skirt. For my basket I needed 77 printed triangles and 77 plain ones. Using the template on page 90 cut out the required quantity of fabric triangles. Referring to the instructions for American Seamed Patchwork on page 129, make a continuous strip of these triangles. Press.

9) Measure the length of the completed patchwork strip and cut a strip of plain polycotton sheeting to the same length and 57 mm (2¼ in) wide. Machine-stitch this strip to the border along its lower edge, i.e. the edge with the plain triangles.

10) Machine-stitch the other edge of the patchwork border to the lower edge of the skirt. Press the seam towards the patchwork. Machine-stitch the centre front seam of the skirt. Press open. Press under a 6 mm (¼ in) turning at the bottom edge of the plain strip below the patchwork. Bring this turn to meet the seam line of the border. Pin and slip-stitch all round. This encloses the raw edges at the back of the patchwork.

11) Stitch 2 lines of gather around the top of the skirt. Draw up the gathers evenly to the same circumference as the top edge of the inner lining of the basket. Pin and tack, right sides together. Machine-stitch, leaving gaps where applicable for the basket handles. Bind the edges of the gaps with bias tape (see instructions on page 137). Sew pieces of ribbon 20 cm (8 in) long at the centre of the gaps left for the handles to tie into bows later on.

12) To fix the completed lining to the basket, stitch tapes firmly to the gathers on the underside of the skirt – 2 at either side of the head and 2 at the foot end. Fit the lining over the basket, attaching it firmly.

Most ready-covered Moses baskets and cots come with a little toy, usually heart-shaped, hanging from the handle or the side – a little soft object for baby to grasp and play with. I thought it nice to pursue the 'watery' theme by making a fish. For a tiny present, you could make it into a pincushion for baby's room.

92

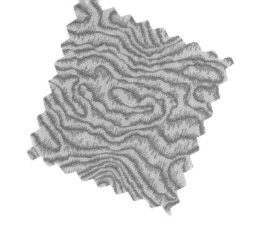

13) The mattress cover. Cut one piece of polycotton using the pattern prepared for the base of the basket. For the base of the mattress, fold the pattern in half and add 5 cm (2 in) to the straight edge. Cut 2 pieces of fabric to this size and stitch a narrow hem along the straight edges. Pin and machine-stitch all around the cover, allowing the 2 hemmed ends to overlap to form an envelope. Turn right side out and press.

14) The lotus quilt. Make a paper pattern approximately 7.5 cm (3 in) wider than the base of the basket and about three-quarters of its length, cutting the top straight across. Allow 15 mm (5/8 in) for the seams. Cut 2 of these shapes from the polycotton sheeting and 1 from the wadding. From 1 of the polycotton pieces, cut off a strip 57 mm (2 1/4 in) wide – this will form the top of the quilt.

15) Apply 3 of the lotus motifs to the quilt top, as described before. Make a strip of patchwork long enough to fit the top straight edge of the quilt. Make up as before. Stitch to the quilt. Press seam towards patchwork.

16) Lay the quilt top and backing on the table, right sides together, with the backing facing up. Place the wadding on top. Pin and tack all 3 layers together. Machine-stitch around the edge, leaving a gap of 20 cm (8 in) on one side. Trim the seam to 6 mm (1/4 in), clip curves and corners. Turn right side out. Slip-stitch opening. Machine-quilt the edge of the patchwork border 'in the ditch' and 6 mm (1/4 in) in from the edge. (See page 136.)

17) The fish. Using the enlarged pattern, cut 2 of each piece. Use the patchwork template to cut the fins (4 triangles in all). Stitch the fins, right sides together, on 2 sides. Turn through to the right side and press. Lay the head and body pieces right sides together at the seam and insert the fin into the centre of the seam, all raw edges matching. Machine-stitch the seam. Repeat for other half of body.

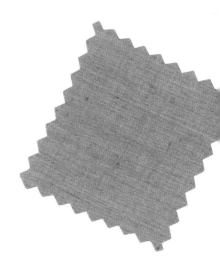

18) With right sides together, machine-stitch all around the fish, leaving a small opening at the side. Trim the seam and clip the corners. Turn right side out, stuff with a little polyester wadding and slip-stitch the opening. Embroider eye and mouth and machine-quilt the lines, as marked.

Playmat with Geese

T he crisp cottons used for this mat give it a clean, fresh look. The instructions will produce a mat measuring approximately 90 cm (36 in) square. If you wish to make a mat to fit inside a playpen, check its dimensions and adjust the measurements and the number of pieces of patchwork accordingly.

YOU WILL NEED

Main colour fabric: 1 m (1¼ yd) of plain cotton or polycotton, 112 cm (45 in) wide

Backing of the mat: 1 m (1¼ yd) of plain contrasting cotton or polycotton, 112 cm (45 in) wide

Medium or heavy-weight polyester wadding: 1 m (1¼ yd) in 96 cm (38 in) width

Main fabric for patchwork border: 50 cm (½ yd) of contrasting plain cotton or polycotton, 90 cm (36 in) width (pale blue in our example)

Appliquéd geese: 25 cm (9 in) of white cotton fabric, 90 cm (36 in) wide

Paper-backed fusible web   Toning threads

Black stranded embroidery thread or black permanent fabric paint

Cardboard for templates

For the patchwork: You will need scraps from about 12 different cotton prints for the border and for the appliquéd bows, small scraps of plain orange-coloured cotton fabric for the geese's beaks and legs. The technique used is American Seamed Patchwork. Look up the instructions on page 129.

The succession of up-ended triangles forms a pattern traditionally known in America as 'flying geese'. Combining this technique with bold appliquéd geese was an obvious choice. The mat measures approximately 90 cm (36 in) square.

N.B. All seam allowances, including patchwork, are 6 mm (¼ in).

1) Using the patterns provided on the opposite page, cut the 2 master templates out of cardboard. You will need 48 of the larger triangles made of printed fabric and 96 small plain ones (pale blue in our example).

2) Arrange your triangles, using 12 patterned and 24 plain for each side of the mat.

3) For the first side of the mat, make 10 patchwork units (see diagram) and join them as per No. 3 on page 130. When these are joined and pressed, measure the length of the strip. Using this measurement for each side, cut a square out of your main fabric for the centre panel. Machine-stitch the patchwork on to the plain square. Press seam towards patchwork.

4) For the second side, join 2 patchwork units together and then a further 10 units in one strip as before. Join the pair of units to one end of the strip as in the diagram opposite. Machine-stitch to centre panel. Repeat for the third side. For side 4, join 10 units with 2 units at either end. Machine-stitch and press.

5) Measure one outer dimension of the patchwork border, cut 4 strips out of your main fabric to that length and 112 mm (4½ in) wide. From the contrasting plain fabric, cut 4 corner squares to the same width. Proceed as per No. 5 on page 66.

6) Enlarge the geese template to 200% and appliqué the pieces as per instructions on page 135. Use matching or toning threads for the satin-stitch embroidery. Hand-embroider the eyes or draw them with black 'permanent' fabric paints, following the manufacturers' instructions. Press the top of the mat carefully.

7) Lay the wadding on a table top and put the backing fabric on top, right side up. Lay the mat face down over it, making sure that there is a small excess of backing and wadding showing all around. Pin and tack together. Trim excess cloth and wadding all around. Machine-stitch 6 mm (¼ in) away from the edge, leaving a 30 cm (12 in)

Cut goose's body in one piece.

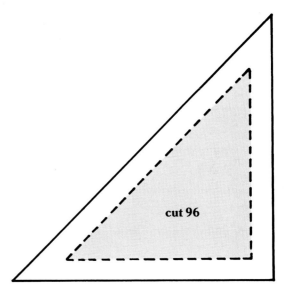

The goose pattern is reproduced half size. Have it enlarged on a photocopier (200%) or trace it on to squared-up dress-making paper. Each large square is equivalent to 50 mm (2 in).

cut 96

Broken line is sewing line.

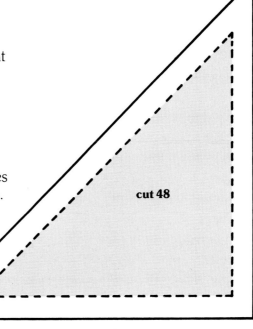

cut 48

opening on one side. Clip corners and trim wadding right up to the seam.

8) Turn the piece right side out, pushing the corners out sharply. Press under the turning and slip-stitch together. Lay the mat on the table, smooth out evenly, then tack at intervals to keep the layers together.

9) With a medium-length machine stitch, quilt 'in the ditch' (refer to No. 3 of page 136) along the border and the corner seams.

10) If you intend to use the mat inside a playpen, attach tapes at appropriate intervals to tie the mat securely to the pen.

Dungarees

These dungarees look equally smart on boys and girls. They are simple and quick to make and if you've never done Crazy Patchwork before, this is a perfect piece to practise on. This garment was designed to fit a child aged between 18 months and 2 years, but its elasticated ankles and the halters which can easily be shortened ensure maximum wear. I have even given you instructions on how to 'customize' a pair of shop-bought dungarees by adding a Crazy Patchwork bib front to them.

YOU WILL NEED

Lightweight polycotton denim: 1 m (1 yd), 90 cm (36 in) wide (this quantity includes bodice lining)

For the patchwork: scraps of toning cotton or polycotton fabric

2 buttons 20 mm (¾ in) wide

2 buttons 12 mm (½ in) wide

Narrow elastic: 50 cm (½ yd)

Matching thread

Contrasting thread for top stitching

Provided you use lightweight fabrics, this outfit could be made entirely out of Crazy Patchwork. You would need the quantity of denim listed above, but of course more of the scraps of toning fabric. By using the pattern, it is easy to work out the quantity of patchwork required to cut the various pieces of the dungarees. Keeping the bib plain, would produce a pleasing contrast.

Little Emma seemed to like her dungarees, but she was not quite sure about the photographic session.

N.B. Seam allowances on the dungarees are 15 mm (⅝ in), except where specified otherwise.

1) Look up instructions for Crazy Patchwork on page 131. Also read the introduction to the Sundress on page 106.

2) Enlarge the pattern on pages 102 to 105 to 200%.

3) Cut a rectangle measuring 40 × 25 cm (16 × 10 in) out of the denim and, using this as your base fabric, work a piece of Crazy Patchwork, following the instructions on page 131. When the piece is complete, lay the enlarged bodice front pattern over it and cut. Cut the remaining pieces of the pattern out of the denim.

4) Fold the straps in half lengthwise and machine-stitch. Bring the seams into the centre of the straps and press open. Machine-stitch along one end of the straps as indicated. Clip corners. Turn right side out and press.

5) Sew straps to the back bodice, matching dots and with raw edges together. Top-stitch along the straps, using contrasting thread, 6 mm (¼ in) from the edges.

6) Lay the back bodice over its lining, right sides together. Pin and machine-stitch all around, leaving an opening at the waist. Clip corners and curves. Trim excess fabric off seams. Turn right side out and press. Repeat this process for the front bodice.

7) Pin and stitch side seams of trousers up to the large dot. Press seams flat. Stitch inside leg seams. Press seam flat.

8) Stitch crotch seam with a double row of stitching for strength. Trim seam and clip curve. Press seam flat.

9) Turn under the extra fabric at the side openings of the trousers so that the edges of the opening meet neatly. Pin and machine-stitch.

10) Gather the waist of the trousers to fit the base of the bodice. Pin the front bodice (do not catch the lining at this stage) to the front of the trousers, right sides together, distributing the gathers evenly. Pin and machine-stitch. Press the seam towards the bodice. Repeat for the back.

11) Turn under 15 mm (⅝ in) along the lower edge of the front and back bodice lining. Press and slip-stitch over the gathers at the waist.

12) Make the buttonholes where indicated and sew on the buttons.

13) Turn up 6 mm (¼ in) at the bottom edge of each trouser leg and press. Turn up a further 38 mm (1½ in) to form a hem. Press, pin and machine-stitch with top-stitching thread, close to the top of the hem. Sew a second line of stitching 6 mm (¼ in) below the first to make a channel for the elastic. Make an opening where the channel crosses one of the side trouser seams and insert pieces of elastic approximately 23 cm (9 in) long – whatever is comfortable for the child. Stitch opening together.

You could also 'jazz-up' a pair of bought dungarees by adding a Crazy Patchwork bib front. Make a paper pattern to the exact size of the existing bib (no need to add a seam allowance). Construct a piece of patchwork large enough to accommodate this pattern and use a piece of plain cotton to form the base of the patchwork. This fabric should be as lightweight as possible in order to avoid making the bib front over thick when finished.

Using the paper pattern, cut the bib out of the patchwork. Lay this on top of the dungaree bib and pin. Attach with a row of stitching, close to the edge. Apply a flat strip of bias binding over the lower edge of the patchwork. Bind the other raw edges of the bib in the usual way (see Dress-making Hints, page 140).

Overleaf. *The pattern on the next 2 spreads is reproduced half size. Enlarge to 200% on a photocopier or trace on to squared-up dress-making paper. The legs of the dungarees were too long to fit on one page, even at the reduced size. You will need to join the 2 sections of the legs after enlarging the pattern.*

Getting used to the bright lights!

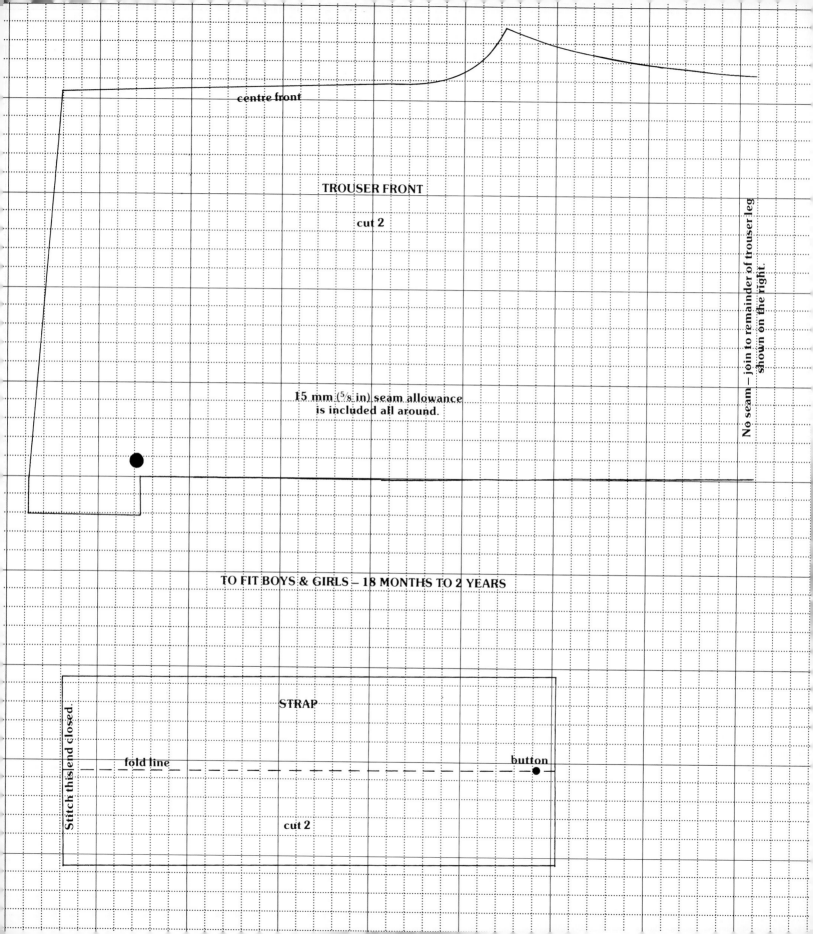

centre front

TROUSER FRONT

cut 2

15 mm (⅝ in) seam allowance
is included all around.

No seam – join to remainder of trouser leg shown on the right.

TO FIT BOYS & GIRLS – 18 MONTHS TO 2 YEARS

STRAP

Stitch this end closed

fold line

button

cut 2

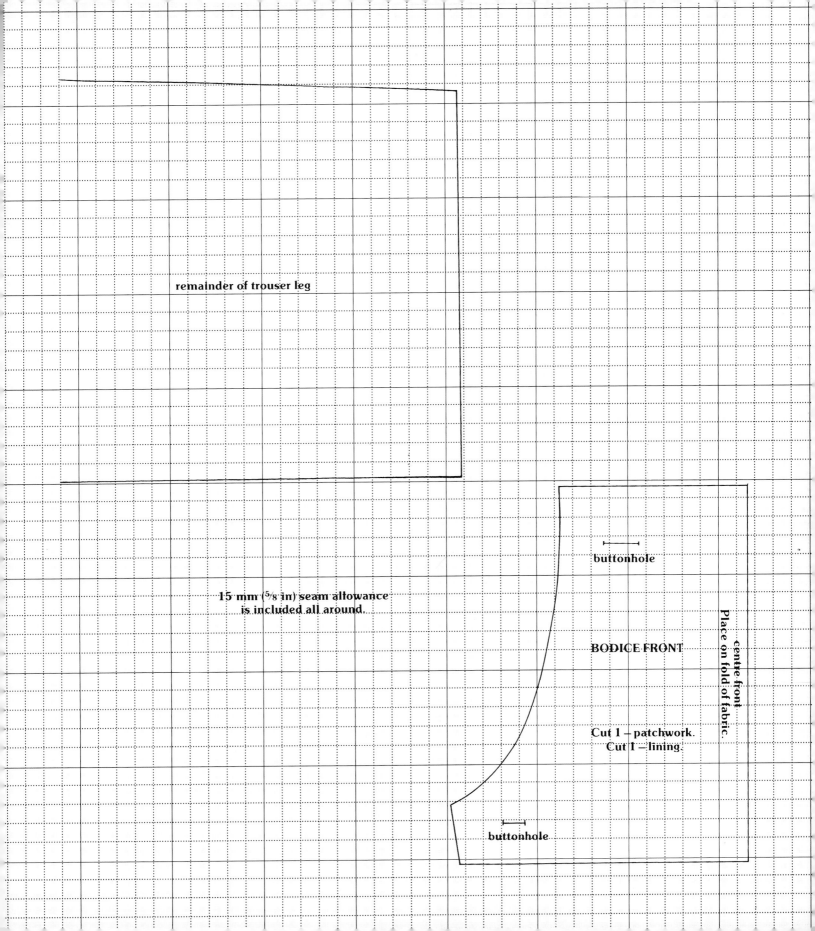

remainder of trouser leg

15 mm (⁵⁄₈ in) seam allowance
is included all around.

buttonhole

BODICE FRONT

centre front
Place on fold of fabric.

Cut 1 – patchwork.
Cut 1 – lining.

buttonhole

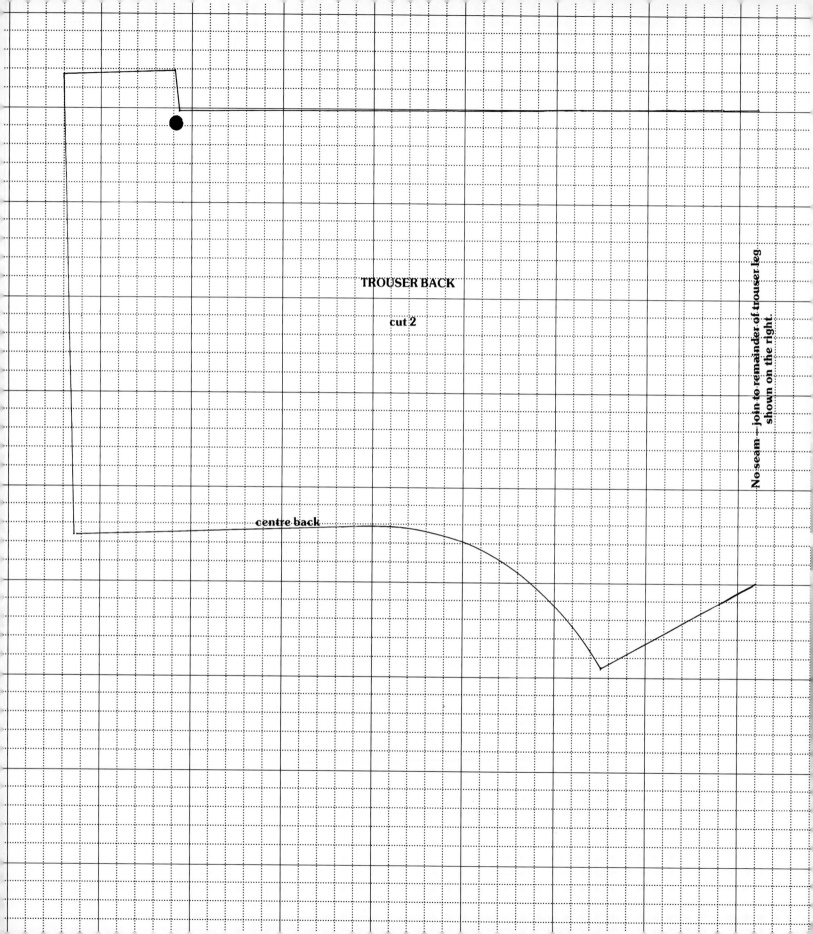

TROUSER BACK

cut 2

centre back

No seam – join to remainder of trouser leg shown on the right.

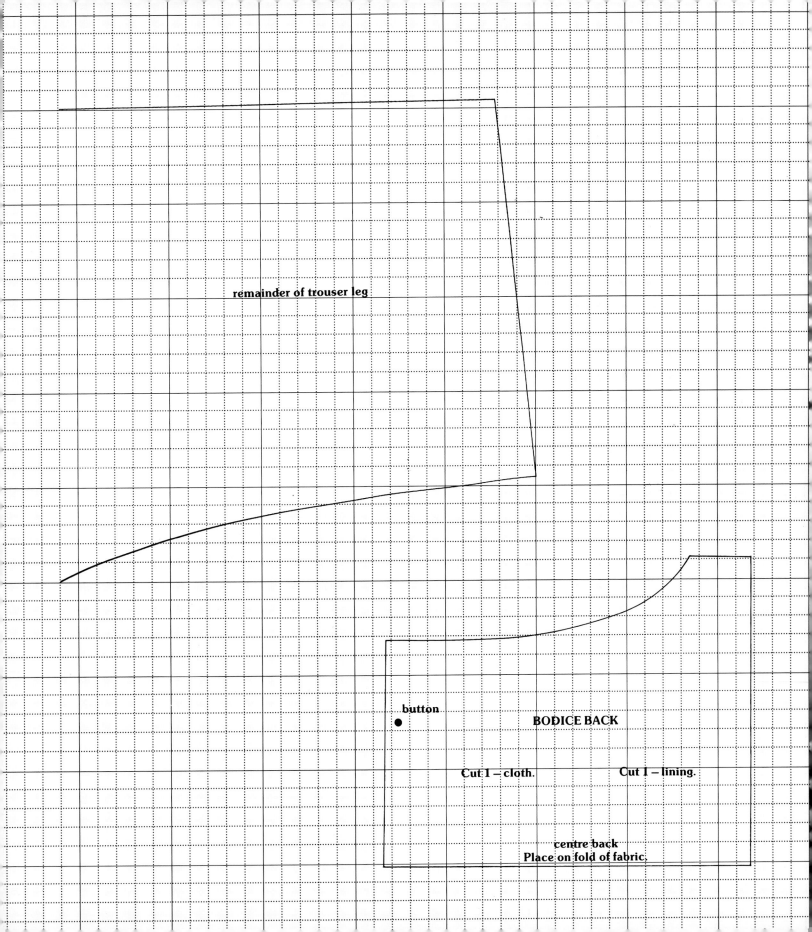

remainder of trouser leg

button

BODICE BACK

Cut 1 – cloth.   Cut 1 – lining.

centre back
Place on fold of fabric.

Sundress

C razy Patchwork is fun to do and uses up the smallest scraps of fabric. I assembled some 12 different patterns for this dress. Look up the instructions for Crazy Patchwork on page 131. Cut the pieces in any shapes you like – keep them small and with straight edges. Traditionally, Crazy Patchwork was done by hand, the pieces often overlapping with the edges left raw. To hide these, an outline of chevron or feather stitch was frequently worked around the pieces. This can also be done with machine-stitched Crazy Patchwork, but I felt that on a small piece like this one, it would become too heavy. This sundress is quick and easy to stitch and assemble, yet it will make an eye-catching outfit for your little girl's first holiday.

YOU WILL NEED

Plain cotton lawn: 1.50 m (1⅔ yd), 90 cm (36 in) wide

For the patchwork: scraps of patterned cotton lawn (12 different patterns have been used in this version)

2 buttons, 13 mm (½ in) wide

Toning thread

The sundress will fit a child aged between 15 months and 2 years.

Rosanna – all ready for the beach! The warm colours of the prints compliment her huge blue eyes and pretty blonde hair.

N.B. Seam allowances on the dress are 15 mm (⅝ in).

1) Cut your patterned cloth in irregular shapes. Keep the edges straight.

2) From the plain cotton lawn cut 1 rectangle measuring 61 × 74 cm (24 × 29 in) and 1 of 51 × 74 (20 × 29 in). Using these as your base fabric, start building up the Crazy Patchwork as described on page 131.

3) Make sure the patch you have just sewn lies nice and flat before adding another one: this will ensure that the finished result is flat and smooth. Cover both lawn rectangles and trim the edges as in No. 4 on page 131. Press flat.

Detail of the top of the dress. The simple loose shape should ensure maximum wear. The dress can also be worn over a T-shirt. Using the same pattern, but making the patchwork out of brushed cottons and needlecord. I made a winter pinafore dress for the little daughter of a friend. The Seminole Jackets on page 81 also show how different garments can be produced out of a single pattern, just by changing the fabric weight.

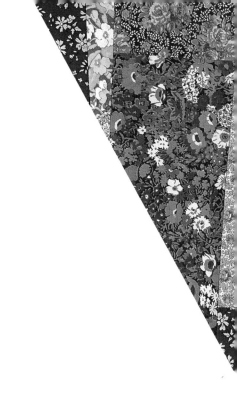

4) Enlarge the pattern shown over pages 110 to 112. You will see that the back of the dress, reproduced on page 110, was too long to fit on 1 page, even at half size. You will need to join the pieces to form the back of the dress, after enlarging the pattern.

5) Take the larger piece of completed patchwork and use it to cut the back of the dress. The second, smaller piece will yield the front of the dress.

6) With right sides together, pin the front to the back of the dress at the sides. Machine-stitch, then neaten seams by hand overcasting or zig-zagging on the machine. Press seams open.

7) Stitch front facing to back facing along the sides.

8) Turn under 6 mm (¼ in) on lower edge of both facings. Press, easing fullness where necessary. Machine-stitch close to the edge.

9) Pin facings to the upper edge of the dress, matching seams. Machine-stitch all around. Trim seams and clip curves.

10) Turn facing to the inside. Press. Catch-stitch the facing to the dress at the seams.

11) Make buttonholes where indicated and sew on buttons.

12) Turn up hem. Tack close to the fold. Trim hem to an even width. Finish raw edge by hand overcasting or with a machine zig-zag. Sew the hem in place, easing in fullness where necessary. Press.

The pattern which begins overleaf is reproduced half size. Each large square on the grid is equivalent to 50 mm (2 in). Enlarge it to 200% on a photocopier or trace it on to squared-up dress-making paper. The back of the dress (page 110), even reduced to half size, was too long to fit in one piece. You will need to join the bottom of the skirt to the top after enlarging the pieces.

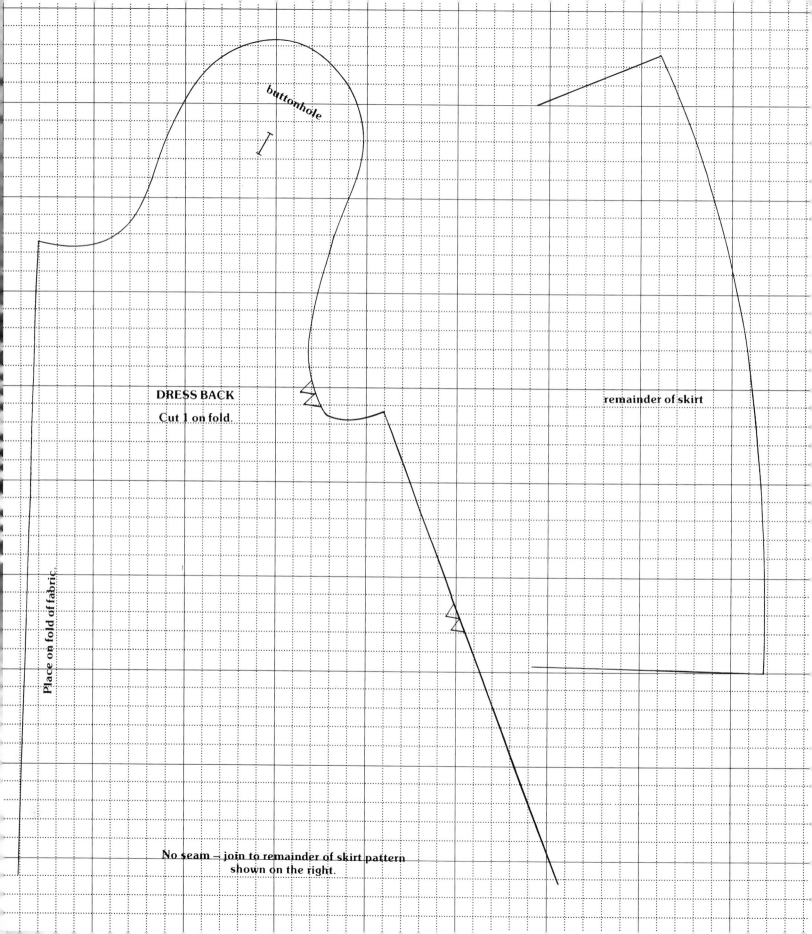

buttonhole

DRESS BACK

Cut 1 on fold.

remainder of skirt

Place on fold of fabric.

No seam – join to remainder of skirt pattern
shown on the right.

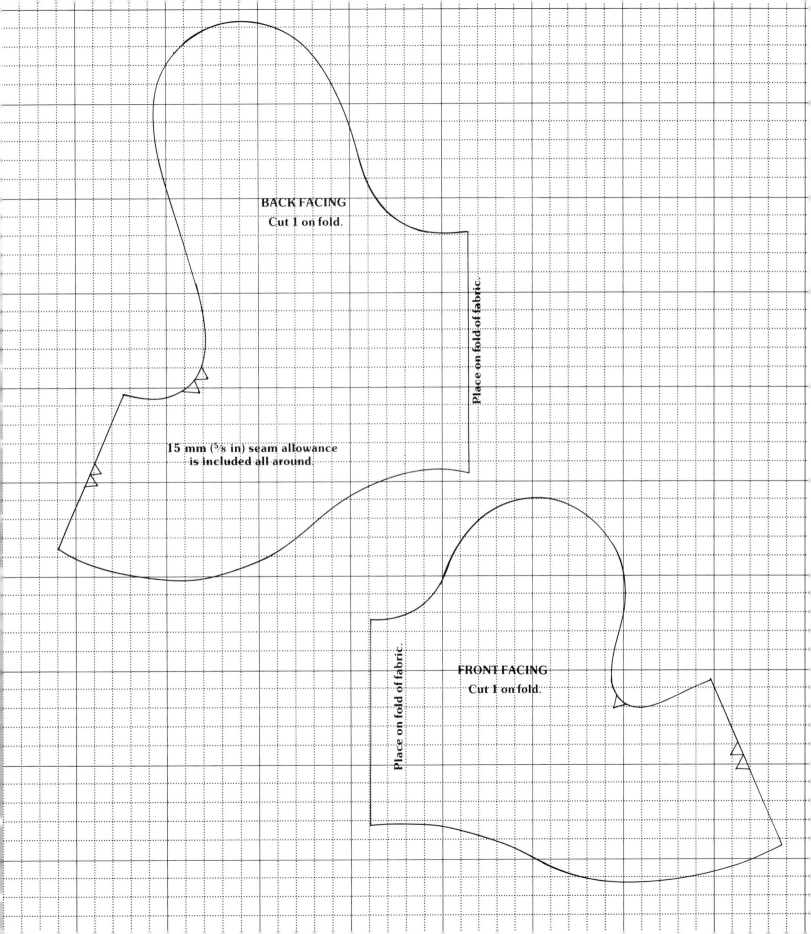

BACK FACING
Cut 1 on fold.

Place on fold of fabric.

15 mm (⅝ in) seam allowance
is included all around.

Place on fold of fabric.

FRONT FACING
Cut 1 on fold.

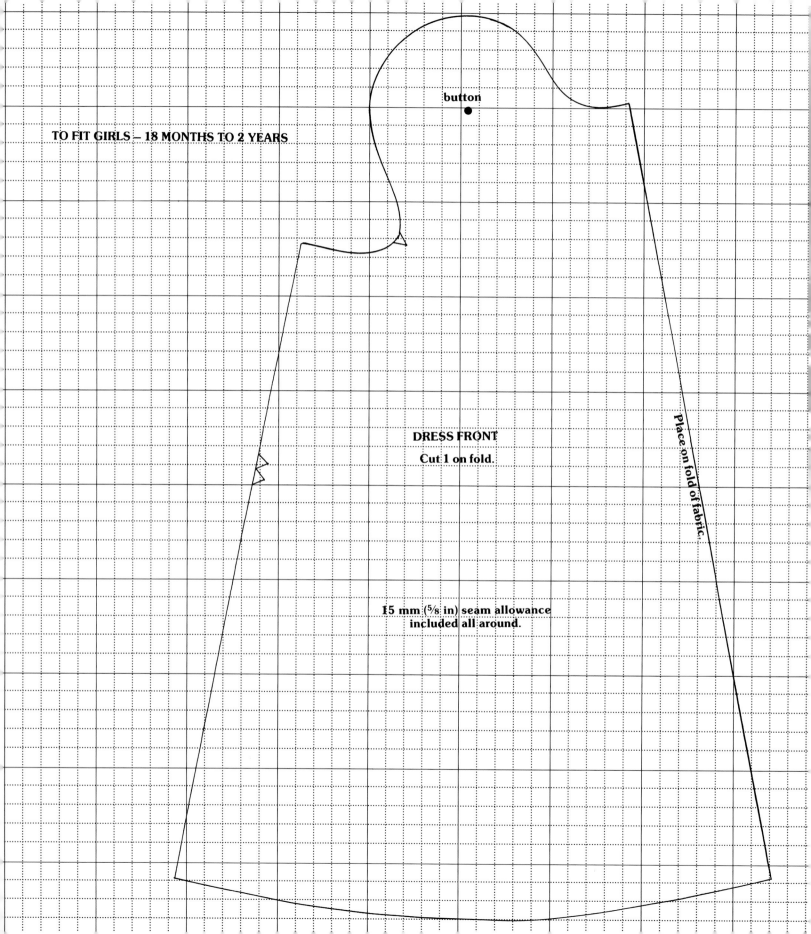

TO FIT GIRLS – 18 MONTHS TO 2 YEARS

button

DRESS FRONT

Cut 1 on fold.

15 mm (⅝ in) seam allowance
included all around.

Place on fold of fabric.

*Peta in all her splendour in the arms of an elegant 'godmother'. The instructions
for the Christening Robe begin overleaf.*

Christening Robe & Bonnet

This elegant christening robe and its bonnet are made of pongee silk which has a lovely, natural deep-cream colour. It is soft, yet has body and an attractive sheen. This is an elaborate garment which is meant as an heirloom, so it is worth investing in a high-quality fabric. The fine lace is machine-made but if you could find antique lace, it would look wonderful. I selected Cathedral Window Patchwork for the borders as its sculptured look gave the dress a vaguely Elizabethan feel. Tiny pearl beads were used at the intersections between the diamonds. I hope you will enjoy making this dress as much as I have.

YOU WILL NEED

Fabric: 3.80 m (4¼ yd) of pongee silk, 122 cm (48 in) wide. Another type of lightweight silk could also be used, or fine cotton lawn.

Lining: 2.60 m (2¾ yd) of silk habotai, 90 cm (36 in) wide

Lace: 2 m (2¼ yd), 70 mm (2¾ in) wide for the hem of the dress and the front of the bonnet

2.50 m (2¾ yd), 25 mm (1 in) wide for the neck, yoke and lower edge of the bonnet

Extra light interfacing: 25 cm (¼ yd)

Ribbon: 1 m (1 yd), 10 mm (⅜ in) wide for the bonnet ties; 25 cm (10 in), 20 mm (¾ in) wide for the flat bow

Elastic: 50 cm (20 in), 3 mm (⅛ in) wide

40 seed pearl beads   2 small buttons

8 tiny satin bows (matching ribbon)   Matching thread

Tailor's chalk or washable fabric marker

The christening robe with its matching bonnet. On page 113 you can see six-month-old Peta wearing the dress.

For the patchwork: for the Cathedral Window centres you will need 50 cm (½ yd) of fine printed cotton or silk. Try to choose a fabric which does not fray too much as it will be easier to work with.

N.B. The seam allowance is 6 mm (¼ in), except where specified differently.

1) To form the base of the patchwork cut a total of 49 – 153 mm (6 in) – squares out of the dress fabric. You will need 10 for the front of the robe, 23 for the edge of the skirt, 5 for each sleeve and 6 for the bonnet.

2) Look up the instructions for Cathedral Window Patchwork on pages 133 and 134. Follow instructions 2) to 6) and make up the patchwork pieces. When you reach stage 6) and bring the 2 corners towards the centre, make sure that the side of the square which has *no seams* in it faces uppermost: otherwise the seams will show in the finished patchwork strip. Complete 39 squares up to stage 6); the remaining 10 should have only one corner folded to the centre. These will form either end of the strips of patchwork. Press lightly.

3) Following instruction 7) on page 134, oversew the units to form one strip each of 6, 10 and 23 pieces, and 2 strips of 5 pieces. Note that each strip should begin and end with one of the special units from which only one corner was folded to the centre.

The detail opposite shows the construction of the Cathedral Window border. As explained on top of page 134, the original squares produced for the patchwork would normally have all 4 corners brought to the centre. Here we have only turned in 2 corners and made a feature of the lower 'points' which come down over the wide lace edging.

template for centres of patchwork

4) Using the template shown on the left, cut 44 'centres' out of your printed fabric. Pin and hand-stitch as in No.8) on page 134. Remember to take into account the fabric pattern and the position the squares will be in when mounted on the dress: avoid flowers growing sideways around the skirt hem, for example.

5) Enlarge the pattern for the robe and bonnet on pages 123 to 127. If you do this on a photocopier, you will need to do it in stages, as a whole side of the dress, for example, will not fit on a sheet. Cut out dress fabric and lining. Note that at this stage you should cut the sleeves out **of the lining only**.

N.B. Wherever possible it is advisable to finish off seams as you go either with a French seam, a self-bound seam or a machine zig-zag (see page 139).

6) The sleeves. Take the 2 strips of patchwork composed of 5 sections and cut 2 oblongs out of the dress fabric to the same length as these patchwork strips and to a width of 18 cm (7 in). Join them on either side of the fabric, mark a 15 mm (⅝ in) seam line along one long side of the plain fabric strip. Use tailor's chalk, a pale coloured pencil or a fabric marker which can be erased easily should any mark be visible after sewing. Test on an offcut of fabric before you begin. Place the Cathedral Window strip with the points of the diamonds butting to the marked seam line. Pin, then machine-stitch carefully along the seam line, making sure that you don't catch the points of the diamonds inside the seam.

7) Neaten the seams either by trimming both layers level (this means cutting off the excess 'points') and zig-zagging over the 2 edges; or by trimming the patchwork points back to a scant 6 mm (¼ in), turning the untrimmed seam allowance of the dress fabric under 3 mm (⅛ in), then turning again to enclose the narrow trimmed edge, bringing the folded edge to the seam line. Slip-stitch in place. Press seams towards the plain fabric.

This is a detail from the edge of the back of the skirt. Note the tiny seed pearls between the diamonds and the way in which the loose 'points' of the Cathedral Window Patchwork form a decorative edging over the deep lace insert.

Use the template on the left to cut the centres of the Cathedral Window Patchwork. Remember to make the best of the pattern in your fabric. The design, whatever it is, should appear like a little picture, framed by the turned down edges of the diamond. See the detail of the border on the page opposite.

8) Using these joined pieces as the fabric for the sleeves, cut the sleeves, positioning the relevant pattern piece carefully and making sure that the patchwork insertion is both centred and straight.

9) Iron on interfacing to the wrong side of the back yoke centre opening. Machine-stitch the back to the front yoke at the shoulders. Press seams open.

10) Machine-stitch the back and the front yokes of the lining at the shoulders. Press seams open.

11) Gather 80 cm (31½ in) of narrow lace with 2 rows of running stitch. Pin the lace all around the yoke, front and back and with right sides together. The straight edge of the lace should lie parallel with the raw edge of the yoke, 13 mm (½ in) away from it. Tack into place, adjusting the gathers evenly. The lace will automatically be sewn on when you join the yoke to the sleeves and to the skirt.

12) Machine-stitch the 2 front side panels to either side of the strip of 10 Cathedral Window units in the same way as you did for the sleeves. Trim and finish as described in No. 7 above. Join the completed front of the skirt to the back of the skirt and do the same with the skirt lining.

13) Measure the strip of Cathedral Window you made for the lower edge of the skirt and cut an oblong of the dress fabric to the same length and 16.5 cm (6½ in) wide. If necessary, cut 2 pieces and seam them together across the width of the strip. Neaten seam and press. This forms what I refer to as the 'lower band'.

14) Along one long edge of the lower band, mark the 15 mm (⅝ in) seam line and, matching centres and with right sides up, lay the long strip of patchwork on to the lower band with the points of the diamonds level with the marked seam line. Pin and tack together.

15) Treating these 2 layers as one, pin to the lower edge of the skirt, right sides together, matching the central Cathedral Window square with the centre of the front of the skirt. Pin the lower band to within 10 cm (4 in) of either side of the skirt centre back seam. Adjust the ends of the lower band so that they meet level with the centre

back seam. Pin, tack and machine-stitch the ends together. Neaten the seam and press. Finish pinning the lower band/patchwork to the edge of the skirt, matching the seams at the centre of the back. Machine-stitch as before, avoiding catching the corners of the diamonds into the seam.

16) Trim the excess patchwork points above the seam line and neaten as in No. 7) on page 117. Allow the bottom points to hang loose over the lower band, where they will form a decorative edge. (See detail of the skirt edge on page 117.)

17) Turn a very narrow hem – 6 mm (¼ in) – at the bottom edge of the lower band, stitching invisibly by hand. By hand or by machine, work a narrow hem at the edge of the skirt lining. If your machine has the capacity, a 'shell edging' looks pretty.

18) Place the lining inside the skirt, wrong sides together. Pin at the side seams, centre back and at intervals around the back part of the waist. Tack the 2 layers together just outside the centre back opening lines. Machine-stitch on the dotted lines, taking 1 stitch across the bottom of the opening. Slash between the stitching.

19) Tack the right side of the continuous lap to the lining side of the back, placing reinforcement stitching on the back along the 6 mm (¼ in) seam allowance on lap. Machine-stitch. Press the seam towards the lap.

20) Turn under 6 mm (¼ in) along the raw edge of the lap and top-stitch over seam on the outside. On the inside bring the ends of the lap together. Machine-stitch diagonally across the lower end of the lap. (Fold the right side of the opening to the inside so that the edges overlap each other.)

21) Run 2 lines of gathers along the back portion of the waist of the skirt and of its lining, treating them as one. Position the first line of gathers at 15 mm (⅝ in) from the raw edge and the second row at 13 mm (½ in) from the raw edge. Repeat for the front of the skirt and its lining, except that you will need to gather these separately, as the front of the skirt is wider than that of the lining.

The back of the dress. The picture shows the opening at the back of the skirt, edged by the 'continuous lap' which is the best method of finishing an opening in a garment where there is no seam. The weight of the Cathedral Window border ensures that the skirt hangs in elegant folds when the baby is carried in the arms of the godmother.

22) Press under a 15 mm (⅝ in) turning to the wrong side, at the base of the back and front of the yoke lining. With right sides together, machine-stitch the yoke and its lining together along the centre back where you fixed the interlining earlier on. Stitch across the pressed turning on the lining.

23) Pull up the gathers at the back of the skirt to fit. Match side seams and place back edges at facing lines. Pin to the backs of the yoke, distributing the fullness evenly. Draw up the gathers of the front of the skirt and of its lining. Distribute them evenly and tack skirt and lining together at the waist. Pin to the front of the yoke, matching centre fronts. Machine-stitch 15 mm (⅝ in) away from the raw edge all around the waist. Run a second line of stitching 6 mm (¼ in) away from the raw edge. Trim the seam allowance close to the second line of stitching. Press the seam towards the yoke, being careful not to press over the gathers.

24) Slip-stitch the lower (folded) edge of the yoke lining over the skirt seam. Tack the yoke and its lining at the neck and sleeve-hole edges.

25) Gather 73 cm (29 in) of the narrow lace, using 2 parallel rows of running stitch. Distribute gathers evenly, then pin and tack the lace to the neck edge, right sides together and with the back edges even.

26) Pin the neck binding to the neck edge (over lace), matching centre fronts, circles to shoulder seams. The ends of the binding should extend beyond the back edges by 6 mm (¼ in). Machine-stitch allowing 6 mm (¼ in) for the seam, stretching the binding to fit. Fold the binding over the seam, turning in the back edges. Turn under 6 mm (¼ in) from the raw edge and hem in place, making sure that the stitches do not come through to the top side of the bodice.

27) The sleeves. Place the straight edge of the lace on the lower edge of the sleeve, right sides together. Tack. Place the sleeve lining over the lace, right sides together. Pin, tack and machine-stitch the lower edge with a 10 mm (⅜ in) seam. Turn right sides out and press so that the lace extends to the very edge of the sleeve. Pin the lining

In the introduction to this project. I suggested that antique lace could be used to trim the dress and the bonnet. Similarly the shape of the bonnet lends itself well to having a family veil, if you own such a thing, being attached from the lower edge, at the back. After use, the robe and bonnet should be professionally dry-cleaned, if necessary, wrapped loosely in acid-free tissue and white calico and folded inside a tightly fitting cardboard box (not a polythene bag). It should be taken out from time to time and shaken out of its folds to prevent the silk from deteriorating along the folds.

to the sleeve at the side edges. Gather the top of the sleeve between the notches with a double row of stitches through both layers.

28) Machine-stitch through both layers along the lines marked to form a channel for the elastic. Cut 2 pieces of elastic 16 cm (6⅜ in) long and thread through the casing, fastening each end of the elastic with 2 or 3 hand stitches. Stitch sleeve side seam, neaten and press.

29) Pin the sleeve into the armhole, right sides together, matching notches, underarm seams and circle to shoulder seam. Pull up gathers, tack and stitch. Stitch again 6 mm (¼ in) away from seam. Trim seam allowances close to the second row of stitching. Neaten and press.

30) Finishing. Make buttonholes in the right side of the back of the yoke, at markings. Lap the right side of the back over the left, matching centres. Mark the position of the buttons and stitch them on.

31) Lay the wide lace flat under the points of the Cathedral Window border at the bottom of the skirt. Slip-stitch the lace on to the lower band so that the lace extends to the edge of the robe and is partly covered by the decorative ends of the patchwork (refer to the picture on page 117). With the larger ribbon form a small flat bow (look at page 117 again) to hide the join between the patchwork diamonds at the back of the skirt. Sew seed pearls at the intersections of the Cathedral Window diamonds. Attach the tiny satin bows at the wrists, the back and front of the yoke, the base of the front patchwork panel and at the back below the larger one (see page 117).

THE BONNET
1) Measure the strip of 6 Cathedral Window pieces you made earlier on and cut 2 pieces of plain silk to the same length – the first one to a width of 80 mm (3⅛ in) and the second one 70 mm (2¾ in) wide.

2) Join the narrower piece to the back edge of the Cathedral Window strip (remember the advice given in No. 4. page 116). Machine-stitch and finish as described in No. 7 of page 117. Press.

This pretty bonnet has elastic at its base, which ensures a good fit. Its soft, enveloping shape will flatter most babies.

3) Along 1 long edge of the second plain strip, mark a 6 mm (¼ in) seam line. With right side uppermost, tack on to it a piece of the wide lace, cut to the same length as the silk strip. The straight edge of the lace should follow the marked seam line on the silk. Treating these as one fabric, join to the front edge of the Cathedral Window strip. Finish and press the seam as before.

4) Lay the completed panel on a table top with the lace facing you. Place the enlarged pattern piece for the bonnet crown – straight edge over the raw edge of the silk panel – which should protrude under the lace. Cut out. Run 2 lines of gathers around the back of the crown and between the notches, at 15 mm and 13 mm (⅝ and ½ in) respectively from the raw edge.

5) Pin the crown to the back of the bonnet, right sides together, matching notches. Draw up the gathering threads to fit. Tack and machine-stitch. Trim seam allowance and neaten. Press seams towards the back of the bonnet. Join lining together.

6) With right sides together, pin and tack the bonnet to its lining, matching notches and seams, pivoting at the corners and leaving a 50 mm (2 in) opening at the back for turning the work. While you machine-stitch, make sure that the front edge of the lace does not get caught in the seam. If necessary make a small pleat at either end across the width of the lace – to avoid this.

7) Turn right side out. Press. Turn in the back opening and tack. Run 1 row of machine-stitching from the front crown strip on one side to that on the other – 6 mm (¼ in) from the bottom edge. Machine-stitch a second row very close to the bottom edge, leaving a small gap. Into this channel, thread 125 mm (5 in) of narrow elastic, anchoring it at either end with 2 or 3 hand stitches. Slip-stitch the gap together. Make a few invisible stitches to anchor the lining to the bonnet at the back seam. Trim the bottom edge of the bonnet with narrow lace and at the centre back, fix a small satin bow. Sew seed pearls at the intersections of the diamonds of the Cathedral Window pattern. Attach 25 cm (10 in) of narrow ribbon to each corner of the bonnet – at circles – to form the ties.

The pattern beginning on the page opposite is reproduced exactly half size. Enlarge it to 200% or transfer it on to squared-up dress-making paper. Each large square is equal to 50 mm (2 in). The dress front on page 124 was too long to reproduce on 1 page, even when reduced. The continuation piece appears on the following page. The same applies to the back of the dress on pages 126 and 127.

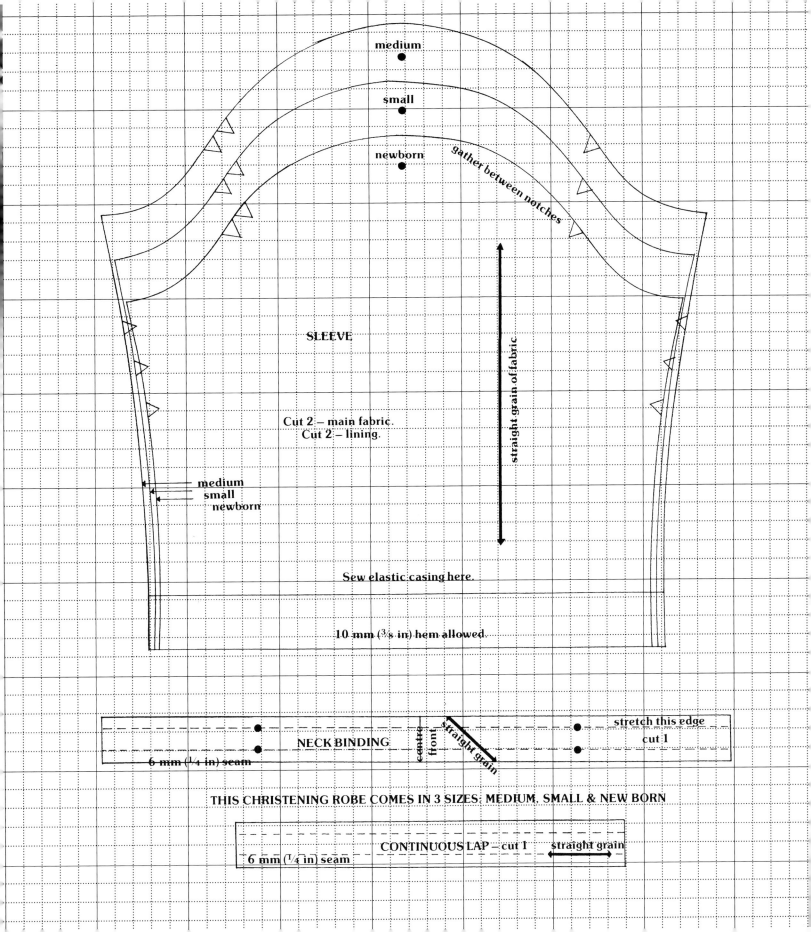

small

newborn

gather between notches

SLEEVE

straight grain of fabric

Cut 2 – main fabric.
Cut 2 – lining.

medium
small
newborn

Sew elastic casing here.

10 mm (³⁄₈ in) hem allowed

NECK BINDING

stretch this edge
cut 1

centre front

straight grain

6 mm (¹⁄₄ in) seam

THIS CHRISTENING ROBE COMES IN 3 SIZES: MEDIUM, SMALL & NEW BORN

CONTINUOUS LAP – cut 1

straight grain

6 mm (¹⁄₄ in) seam

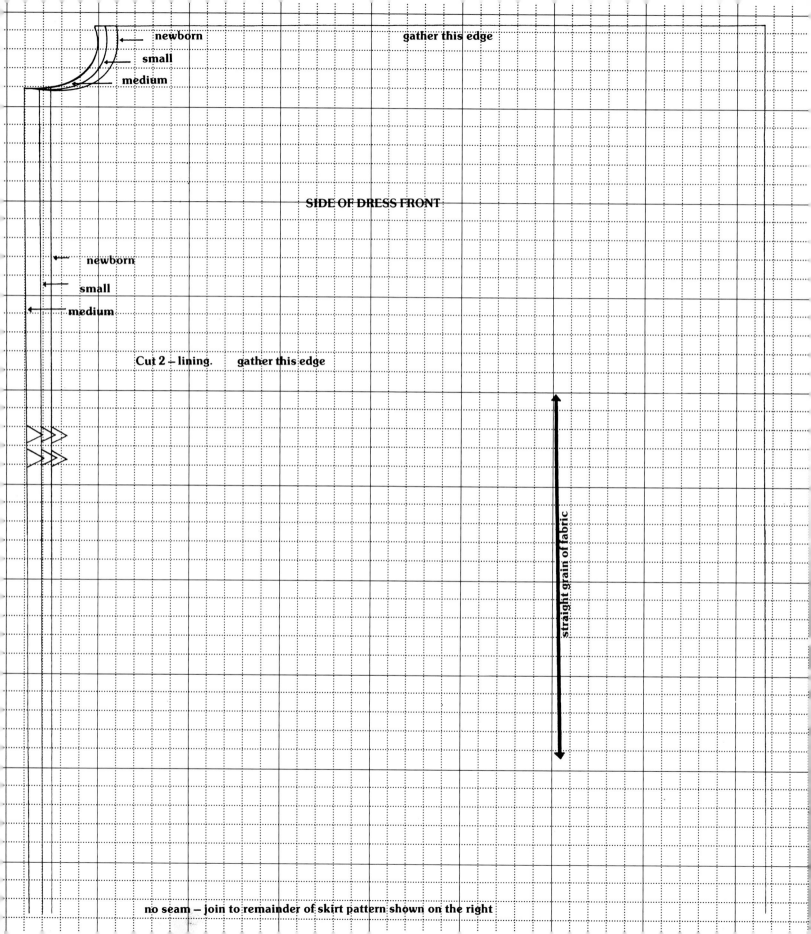

newborn

small

medium

gather this edge

SIDE OF DRESS FRONT

newborn

small

medium

Cut 2 – lining.   gather this edge

straight grain of fabric

no seam – join to remainder of skirt pattern shown on the right

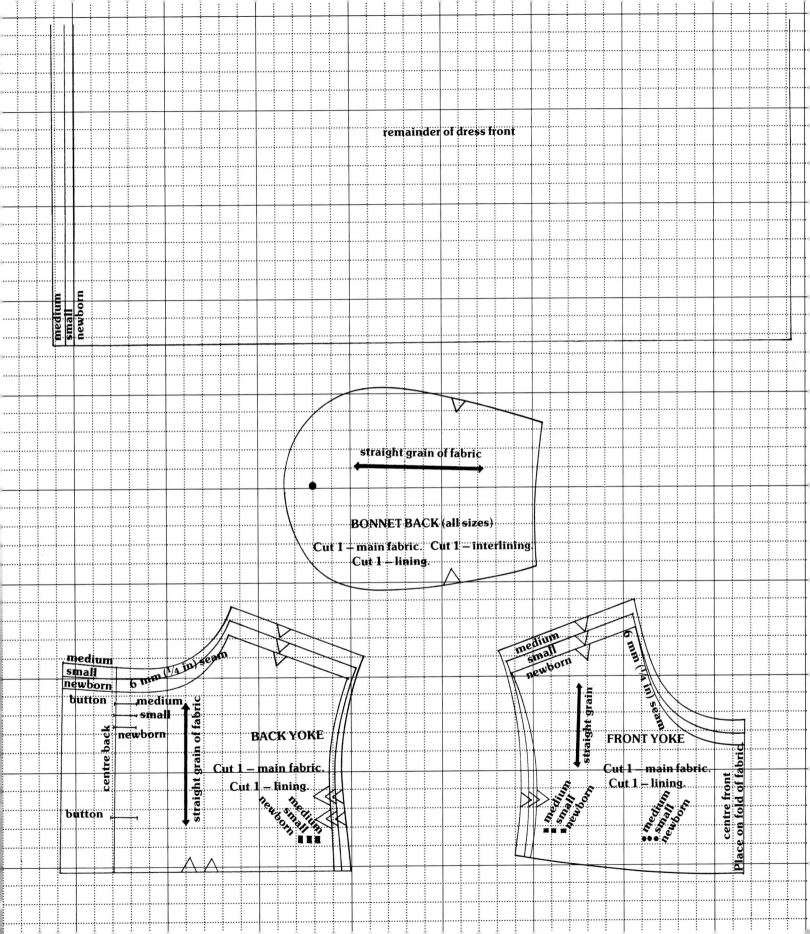

remainder of dress front

medium
small
newborn

straight grain of fabric

BONNET BACK (all sizes)
Cut 1 – main fabric. Cut 1 – interlining.
Cut 1 – lining.

medium
small
newborn
6 mm (1/4 in) seam

button

medium
small
newborn

centre back

straight grain of fabric

BACK YOKE
Cut 1 – main fabric.
Cut 1 – lining.

medium
small
newborn

button

medium
small
newborn

medium
small
newborn
6 mm (1/4 in) seam

straight grain

FRONT YOKE
Cut 1 – main fabric.
Cut 1 – lining.

medium
small
newborn

centre front
Place on fold of fabric

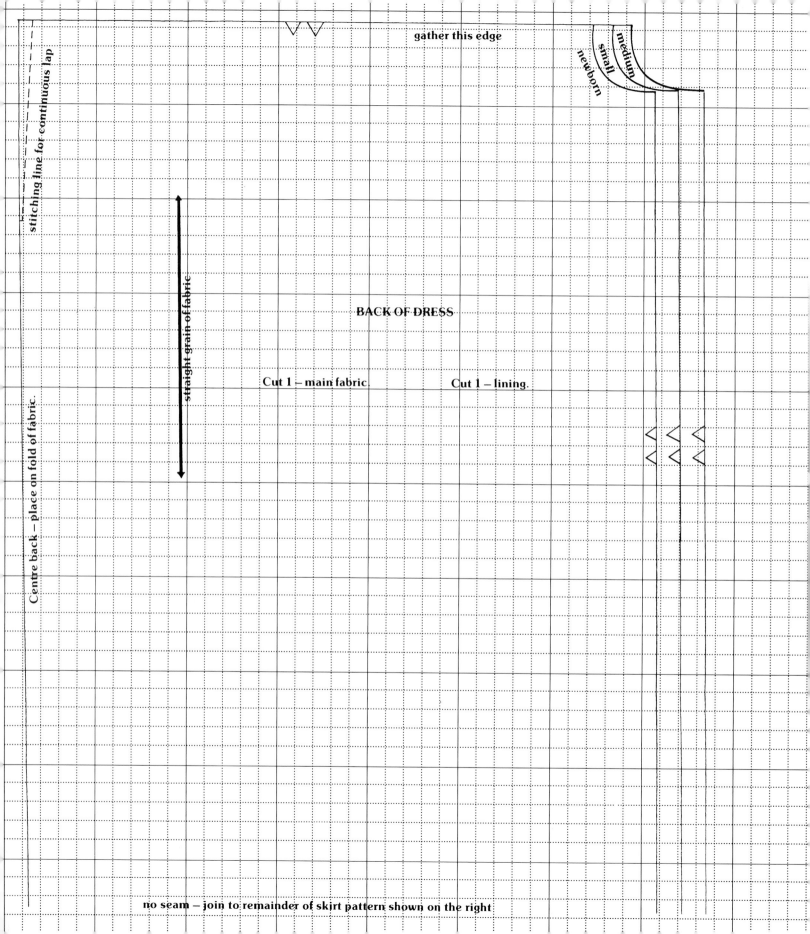

gather this edge

stitching line for continuous lap

newborn
small
medium

Centre back – place on fold of fabric.

straight grain of fabric

BACK OF DRESS

Cut 1 – main fabric.   Cut 1 – lining.

no seam – join to remainder of skirt pattern shown on the right

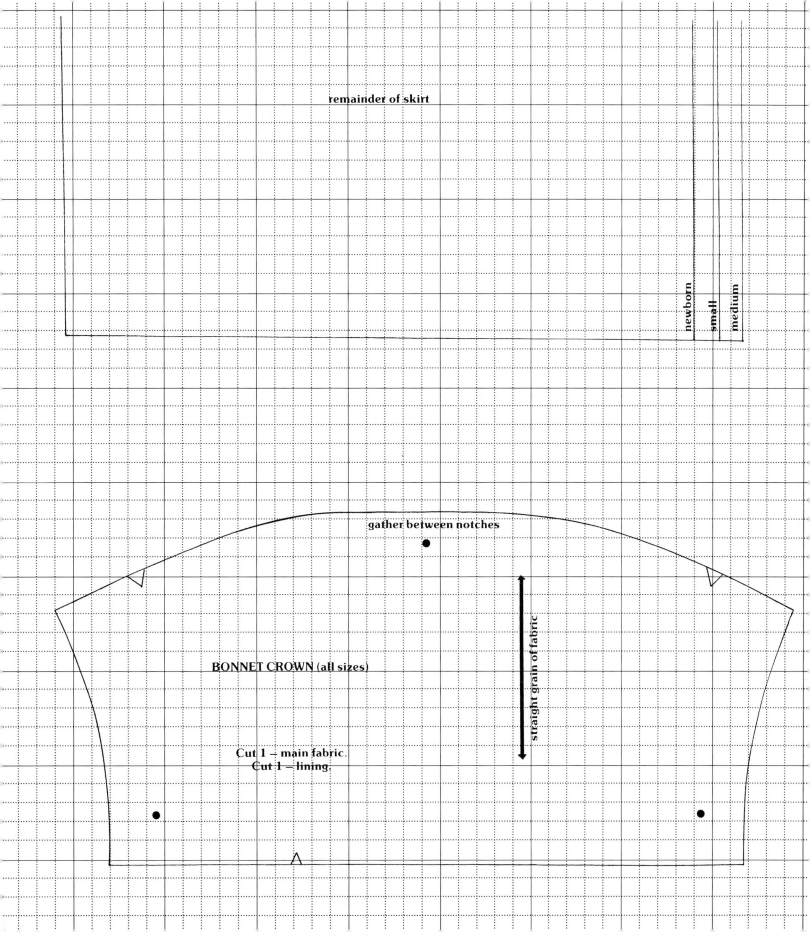

remainder of skirt

newborn

small

medium

gather between notches

straight grain of fabric

BONNET CROWN (all sizes)

Cut 1 — main fabric.
Cut 1 — lining.

Patchwork Techniques

ENGLISH PATCHWORK

English Patchwork is sewn by hand. Paper templates must be cut to the exact size of the finished patchwork pieces. This is done by using a master template made of cardboard or bought ready made. The cloth is cut, leaving a seam allowance all around, and tacked on to the paper templates. English Patchwork uses one basic shape – a square, a hexagon, a diamond or other – throughout a given piece. The patches are oversewn, right sides together – see No. 1 below – with tiny regular stitches which should not catch through the paper. Toning thread is mostly used. The patchwork is pressed with the paper templates still in place and these are only removed when the piece is ready for mounting.

1)

2)

3)

1) Master template, prepared patches tacked on to their paper templates and 2 patches being stitched, working from right to left. It is important to catch only a couple of threads from the cloth on each side.

2) Finished patches with the tacking and templates still on. The stitches should hardly show at all on the right side.

3) The back of the piece of patchwork after pressing. The tacking and paper templates have now been removed.

DRESDEN PLATE PATCHWORK

The projects in this book use an adaptation of the Dresden rosette which has elongated segments, arranged concentrically, around a circular appliquéd piece.

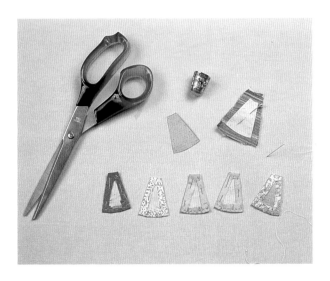

Dresden Plate Patchwork is hand-sewn. It is made in the same way as English Patchwork, using an accurately cut master template and paper templates. The difference lies in the treatment of the curved edge along which the fabric must be slightly gathered to eliminate the fullness and then tacked in the usual way. The patches are then oversewn in the same manner as for English Patchwork. Remove the tacking gradually, as the curved edges could easily lose their shape.

AMERICAN SEAMED PATCHWORK

1)

2)

1) Using the width of the presser foot as a guideline for the seams, join 3 pieces to form a complete unit, see No. 2.

2) A finished unit. Complete as many as you need, finger-press, then join the units together.

3)

3) A finished length of American Seamed Patchwork border. This pattern is known as 'flying geese' and it was used for the border on the Playmat described on page 94.

Nowadays, American Seamed Patchwork is made on the machine and it is an effective and relatively quick method to produce spectacular quilts. It can be sewn by hand, using a running stitch and no paper templates.

LOG CABIN

Log Cabin Patchwork consists of narrow strips arranged around a centre square. The pieces are fixed on to a patch of white fabric on which sewing lines have been marked. The figures – 1, 2, 3 and 4 – are there to remind you to work clockwise. Half of the block is worked in light fabrics and the other half in dark.

1)

2)

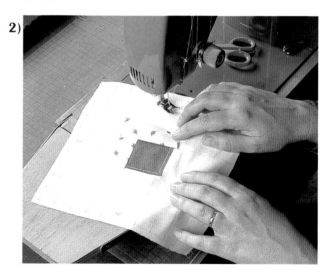

1) The square of white cloth has been marked, using a washable fabric marker. The centre square goes first, followed by the first strip. This form of patchwork was used for the bag and mat on page 72.

2) The first strip has been finger-pressed and the second has been added. The latter has been turned down and the work is now ready for the next strip to go along the third side of the square.

CRAZY PATCHWORK

1)

3)

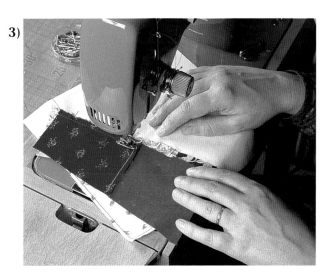

Crazy Patchwork uses random pieces. It is now frequently made on the machine. In this case the patches must have straight, *not* curved edges.

2)

4)

1) Apply the first patch in a corner of the base fabric. Machine-stitch as shown.

2) 2 patches have been joined together and are now being added as a single piece.

3) Joining another unit. Do not trim off the ends. Cover the whole piece first.

4) Finished piece with edges trimmed off. Treat as one fabric and cut to shape.

SEMINOLE PATCHWORK

This clever technique was developed by a tribe of native Americans when they were first introduced to the sewing machine. This technique was used for the jackets on page 80.

1)

3)

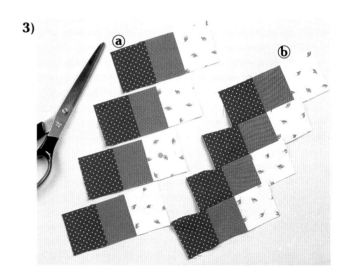

2)

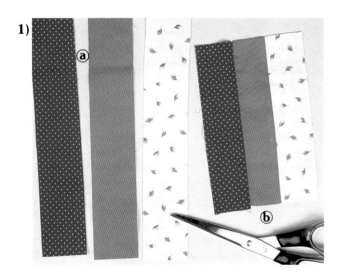

4)

1) Cut 3 strips ⓐ, then machine-stitch ⓑ.

2) Draw lines at right angles across the sewn strips. The spacing is equal to the width of the original strips. Cut.

3) Re-align pieces ⓐ, and stitch together ⓑ.

4) Draw a line on either side of diamonds, leaving a 6 mm (¼ in) seam allowance and cut as shown. The strip is now ready.

CATHEDRAL WINDOW

This method was used to produce the borders on the Christening Robe on page 114. It combines machine- and hand-sewing.

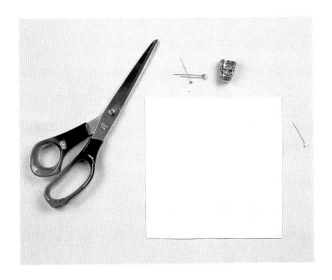

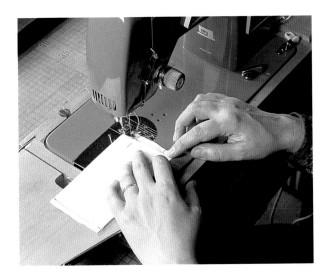

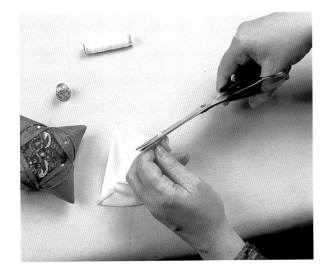

1) Cut the basic square (size given with project).

2) Fold square in half, machine-stitch down one side, repeat for the other as shown.

3) Press seam open and trim corners. Repeat. Fold pocket across to form a square. Pin the open side, as shown.

4) Machine-stitch second seam, leaving small gap. Press seam, trim corners.

If you were producing a piece of Cathedral Window Patchwork, rather than a strip, all 4 corners of the little squares would need to be brought to the middle (rather than the 2 shown in No. 6 below). This would form a smaller square. N.B. The little coloured centres are cut without a seam allowance.

5)

7)

6)

8)

5) The square has been turned out and the small gap slip-stitched closed.

6) Bring 2 of the corners towards the centre and anchor-stitch (side without seams uppermost).

7) Join 2 shapes along folded sides, oversew.

8) Pin coloured centres, turn down the plain coloured edges over the raw ones of the coloured squares. Hem-stitch neatly.

APPLIQUÉ

Using template, draw required shapes on to the paper backing of the
fusible material.

1)

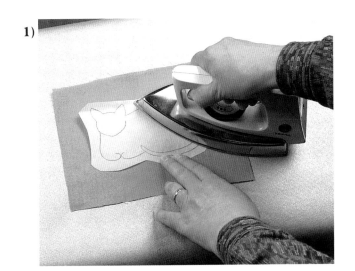

3)

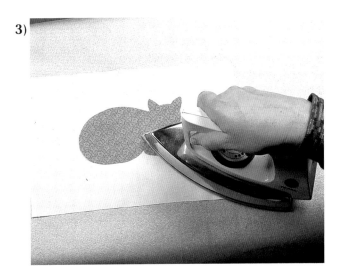

2)

4)

1) Fusible material being ironed on to the
   wrong side of the fabric.

2) Cut accurately around the drawn shape
   and remove the paper backing.

3) Place shape, adhesive side down, over
   the base fabric and press as shown.

4) Satin-stitch around the edges as shown.
   Details such as the cat's features are
   then worked by hand in stem-stitch.

QUILTING

The original purpose of quilting was to hold several layers of fabric together to produce a warm covering. The technique can be used to produce designs of amazing complexity and beauty.

1)

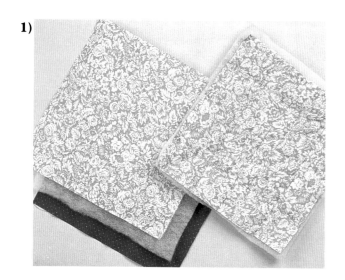

3)

2)

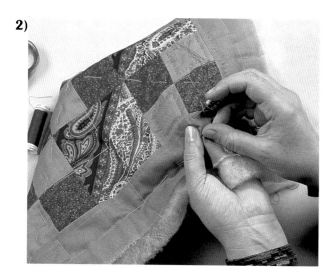

Both hand and machine-quilting have been used in this book. The little quilt on page 64 is hand-quilted, away from the seams. The Playmat with the geese motif on page 94 was quilted in 'the ditch'. American Hamish quilts, for example, can appear very austere, using only 2 or 3 plain contrasting fabrics but all the craftsmanship and the fantasy of the maker were given free rein in the quilting. They often present the most intricate and attractive designs. The quilting bees were, and still are, an important part of the social life of many women in America.

1) The back of the quilt, the wadding and the top of the quilt are tacked together.

2) Hand-quilting, away from the seam. If you need a guideline, use tailor's chalk, tracing as you go along.

3) Quilting 'in the ditch', i.e. into the seam line on the sewing machine.

BINDING & MITRING

The golden rule is to use a strip 6 times the finished
width of the bound edge.

1)

3)

2)

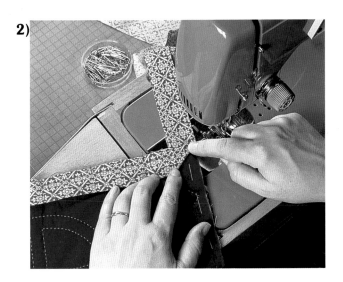

4)

1) The cut strip is folded over as shown.

2) Starting from the centre of 1 side and
   working on the top side of the quilt,
   machine-stitch up to the seam allowance.
   Fold the strip along the diagonal.

3) Fold corner as shown and machine-stitch
   down the 2nd side. Repeat all around.

4) Back of the quilt. Fold strip over and
   slip-stitch, mitring the corner as shown.

Dress-making Hints

There are many books available which give detailed, step-by-step dress-making instructions and which cover all the processes involved in the production of various garments. The purpose of this short section is merely to explain the terms and processes referred to in this book and which have not been explained in relation to individual projects.

N.B. Throughout the book, unless otherwise stated, seam allowances for the patchwork are 6 mm ($\frac{1}{4}$ in) and 15 mm ($\frac{5}{8}$ in) for dress-making purposes.

TACKING. The purpose of this stitch is to hold 2 or more layers of fabric together, for fitting or for stitching. It is used when pins alone are unsuitable i.e. if you need to try on the garment, or if pinning is not sufficient to hold the pieces of fabric in the correct position for stitching. Use tacking thread rather than ordinary thread as it is easier to break and pull out after the stitching has been completed. Tacking is done by taking several running stitches on to the needle before pulling it through the fabric. The size of the stitches should be approximately 6 mm ($\frac{1}{4}$ in) to 12 mm ($\frac{1}{2}$ in) in length on ordinary sewing, but can be anything from 25 mm (1 in) to 38 mm ($1\frac{1}{2}$ in) long when tacking layers together for quilting, see No. 1 of page 136, for instance.

SLIP STITCH. An almost invisible stitch used for hemming and hand appliqué. Work from right to left, holding the folded edge in your left hand. Bring the needle up through the fold. Take a stitch into the cloth, directly opposite from where the thread came out, catching just 1 or 2 threads. Slip the needle into the fold at a distance of about 6 mm ($\frac{1}{4}$ in). Continue taking stitches at 6 mm ($\frac{1}{4}$ in) intervals. Slip-stitching is much used in dress-making for closing the gaps left in a seam to turn the garment inside out, for example.

STAY-STITCHING. On the sewing machine, run a line of stitching 13 mm ($\frac{1}{2}$ in) from the raw edge (within seam allowance). This is often done around the neck of a garment before finishing the neck or mounting a collar, for instance, in order to prevent the cloth from fraying and the neckline from losing its shape.

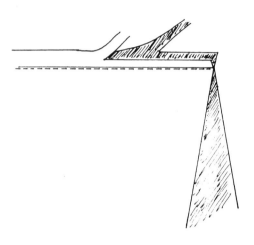

layering a seam by trimming one side shorter than the other

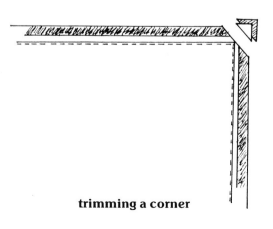

trimming a corner

TRIMMING OF SEAMS. The heavier the fabric, the more important it is to trim to reduce the excess fabric and lose the unsightly bulk. One method is **layering**. The diagram opposite left shows how it is done. The fabric is trimmed to different heights along both seam allowances. It is important not to trim too short, but this is a useful method with thick woollen materials. **Trimming corners.** When you have seams meeting at a right angle, the corner must be trimmed so that it can be fully pushed out when the work is turned to the right side. Care must be taken not to trim too short. **Clipping inner curves.** This operation will ensure that the armhole or the neck of a garment lies smoothly (*see diagram*). **Notching outer curves.** This will be done around a collar, for instance. The seam allowance is first trimmed short, then notched.

**cutting notches
in an outer curve**

GATHERING. This is done by machining a row of long stitches on the seam line, followed by a second row within the seam allowance, 6 mm (¼ in) from the first row. Loosen the upper tension slightly before stitching. It is then easier to pull the gathers to fit. To gather, pull up the bobbin threads. Adjust the gathers to the required length and anchor firmly at both ends. Gathering can also be done by hand by running 2 parallel rows of running stitch as described above. Adjust the length and finish off as above.

SEAM FINISHES. Unless a seam is to be permanently covered, as in the edges of a quilt for instance, the wrong side of a seam has to be neatened in some way. The simplest method on a firm fabric is to trim the seam edges with pinking shears. A **zig-zag finish**, if your machine has this setting, is a good way to finish off a garment. It is worked near to but *not* over each edge of the seam allowance. You then have to trim close to the zig-zag, taking care not to cut into the stitching. Another alternative is to work a **self-bound seam.** This begins with a plain seam of which *one* seam allowance is trimmed down to 3 mm (⅛ in). The untrimmed allowance is turned under 3 mm (⅛ in) then turned again, enclosing the narrow trimmed edge and bringing the folded edge to the seam line. Stitch along the folded edge, as close as possible to the first line of stitching. Press seam to one side. A **French seam** is produced by sewing the wrong sides of the fabric together and stitching 10 mm (⅜ in) from the edges on the right side of the fabric. Trim the seam allowance to 3 mm (⅛ in). Fold right sides together, with stitching line exactly on the fold. Press flat. Stitch 6 mm (¼ in) from the fold. This step

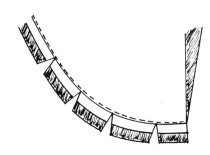

clipping inner curves

encases the cut edges. Check that no loose threads are showing on the right side of the work. Trim if necessary and press the seam to one side. Both self-bound and French seams produce a very strong as well as a neat finish.

ZIP FASTENERS. To insert a centred zip fastener, stitch the seam up to where the fastener will reach. Pin the seam together and tack closed on the seam line. Press the seam flat and mark where the fastener will reach to. Working from the wrong side, place the zip fastener face down on the seam, over the tacked section. Pin and tack into place, keeping the teeth of the zip over the seam line. On the right side of the work, mark the bottom of the zip with a pin and stick a length of 13 mm (½ in) wide transparent tape, to the same length as the zip and down the centre of the seam line. Using a zipper foot on your sewing machine and the edge of the sticky tape as a guideline, stitch down one side of the fastener. Stitch down the other side in the same way, pivoting at the end of the line of stitching and sewing across the end of the zip. Finish stitching with a backstitch then pull all the threads to the wrong side and knot close to the fabric. Remove tacking and press.

BUTTONHOLES. Generally a buttonhole should be 3 mm (⅛ in) longer than the button but it is always advisable to make a test buttonhole on a spare piece of fabric, before attempting the real thing. Make sure that your test piece is layered in the same way as the portion of the garment on which the buttonhole will eventually come. If you have an automatic buttonholer on your sewing machine, follow the instructions given. When you cut the buttonhole open, place a pin at either end of the buttonhole, in front of the bar tacks, to avoid cutting through the ends. Use the point of small sharp scissors or a seam ripper, cutting from the centre of the buttonhole towards one end, then the other. If you make the buttonhole by hand, the hole should be cut first and the edges overcast (loose oversewing stitches) to prevent the edges from fraying. The buttonhole stitches are then worked from left to right, very close together.

BIAS BINDING. To apply commercial bias binding to the raw edges of a garment, open one edge of the binding and lay it on the garment with right sides together and raw edges matching. Pin and tack into position. Stitch on the fold line of the bias tape, folding under and overlapping the ends if necessary. When this is complete, fold the bias tape to the wrong side of the fabric, enclosing the raw edges, and slip-stitch into place.

HEMS. Hems may be machine-stitched, especially where only a narrow hem is required. Care must be taken to ensure that the stitching is straight as it will be visible on the garment, but on a delicate piece of work, it is well worth taking the time to hand-stitch the hems. On a garment with a flared hem, the fullness should be controlled by gathering the hem slightly. Run gathers 6 mm (¼ in) from the raw edge, pin the hem to the garment and draw up gathering thread slightly. Press carefully then sew bias binding over the gathering. Pin and tack the hem to the garment and finish with a blind hemming stitch – that is a very small stitch inside the edge of the hem fold, picking up one thread of the fabric before taking another stitch on the inside of the hem fold. Do not pull the thread taut. Press carefully.

TOP STITCHING. This is a line of decorative stitching worked some 6 mm – 10 mm (¼–⅜ in) away from the edge, using a medium-sized machine-stitch, with the right side of the work uppermost. It can be made in toning or contrasting thread.

PRESSING. This is an all-important operation in dressmaking and you should really have the iron at the ready at all times as seams should be pressed as you go along. Similarly, many of the machine-stitched forms of patchwork described in this book call for the pressing of seams in stages. Always remember to push the seams under the patchwork as they could show through the work. It is a lesson many of us have learnt the hard way! Many of the projects in this book include silks among the fabrics: remember that some types of silk, although perfectly washable, will mark if they come in contact with *droplets* of water – even a steam iron may cause problems. If you wash them, they must not be allowed to dry completely, but should be pressed while still damp. Silks can withstand very high temperatures and can be pressed at a much higher setting than generally recommended by the markings on your iron. There are various brands of sprays (not starch) on the market which are useful when pressing silks and other fine fabrics. They restore body and ease out the creases in the cloth. Always make sure that your iron is perfectly clean before you use it on delicate fabrics.

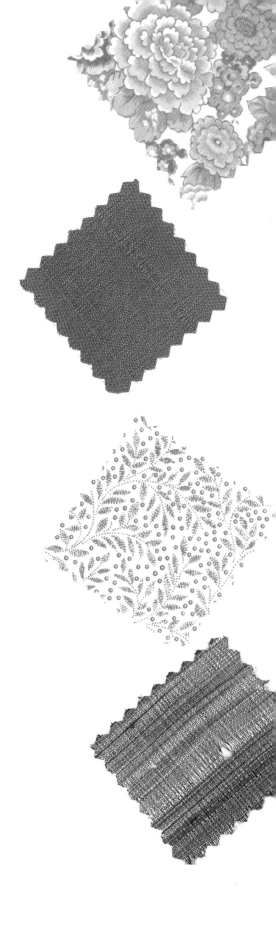

141

List of Suppliers

John Lewis plc, Oxford Street, London W1A 1EX (general fabrics and haberdashery)

Liberty plc, Regent Street, London W1R 6AH (fine fabrics and haberdashery)

Harrods Ltd, Knightsbridge, London SW1X 7XL (fine fabrics and haberdashery)

Pongees Ltd, 184-186 Old Street, London EC1V 9FR (silk fabrics – mostly plain)

The Thai Silk Shop in Tenterden, 104 High Street, Tenterden, Kent TN30 6HT (silk fabrics – small amounts suitable for patchwork)

Strawberry Fayre, Chagford, Devon TQ13 8EN. Mail order only. (cotton fabrics – special 'Amish' range)

Village Fabrics, Lester Way, Wallingford, Oxfordshire OX10 9DD (cotton fabrics)

The Country Store, 68 Westbourne Road, Marsh, Huddersfield, W Yorkshire. Also mail order.

Crimple Craft, 1 Freemans Way, Forest Lane, Wetherby Road, Harrogate, Yorkshire HG3 1RW. Also mail order. (American & English cotton fabrics)

Green Hill, 27 Bell Street, Romsey, Hampshire SO51 8GY. Also mail order.

Piecemakers, 13 Manor Green Road, Epsom, Surrey KT19 8RA. Also mail order. (large range of fabrics)

The Quilt Room, 20 West Street, Dorking, Surrey RH4 1BL. Also mail order. (fabric – quilting supplies)

Organizations

National Patchwork Association, PO Box 300, Hethersett, Norwich, Norfolk NR9 3DB (tel: 0603 812259)

The Quilters' Guild, Unit P66, Dean Clough, Halifax, West Yorkshire HX3 5AX (tel: 0422 347669). Publish a quarterly full-colour magazine which is sent to members.

Both previously named organizations will put inquirers in touch with local patchwork/quilting groups.

Patchwork Guild of Northern Ireland, C/o Irene MacWilliam, 67 Drumberg Road, Dunmurry, Belfast, Northern Ireland BT17 9LE

The Crane Gallery, 171a Sloane Street, London SW1X 9QG (display & sale of quilts)

The American Museum in Britain, Claverton Manor, Bath, Avon BA2 7BD (permanent exhibition of fine early American quilts)

Bibliography

Fairfield, Helen: Patchwork (Batsford, 1990)

Guerrier, Katherine: The Quilting and Project Book (The Apple Press, 1992)

Seward, Linda: The Complete Book of patchwork. Quilting and Appliqué (Mitchell Beazley, 1987)

Singer Sewing Reference Library – Quilting by Machine (Cy De-Cosse Inc, 1990)

Travis, Dinah: The Sampler Quilt Workbook (Batsford, 1990)

Index